MW00389512

The sacred name of God, Yahweh, is indicated by "Lord."

ISBN 0-9628971-9-1

Second Edition © 2006

To receive our bimonthly magazine, *The Sower*, and a complete listing of our materials contact us at:

Christian Educational Services
A division of Spirit & Truth Fellowship International
2144 East 52nd Street
Indianapolis, IN 46205
888.255.6189 (317.255.6189), M-F 8:30 to 5 (EST)
Fax: 317.255.6249
STF@STFonline.org
www.STFonline.org

For further study, please visit our research website:

www.TruthOrTradition.com

Dedicated to helping you understand the Word of God, free from the traditions of men.

Printed in the United States of America.

TABLE OF CONTENTS

CHAPTER ONE
Some Basics About Prophecy

Hearing from God. What could be more important or wonderful than that? Through the ages, prophecy was a primary way that people heard from God.[1] It has been very important to God and His people from Genesis until now, and will continue to be important through the book of Revelation. Prophecy is also one of the ways in which the Lord Jesus Christ works in the Church. Prophecy is one of the spiritual things that we Christians are to "especially" understand and utilize:

1 Corinthians 14:1 (NKJV)
Pursue love, and desire spiritual *gifts,* but especially that you may prophesy.

The purpose of this book is to give Christians a basic understanding of the manifestation of prophecy. Therefore, it will focus on things that are usually encountered in corporate (to groups) and personal (to individuals) prophecy, and will not go into depth about things that are more generally revealed to those who have the ministry of a prophet.

What is Prophecy?

The answer to the question, "What is prophecy?", is of utmost importance, and so for clarity it is answered in four parts below.

---

1. Throughout this book, "God" refers to God, "the Lord" refers to the Lord Jesus Christ, and "LORD" is the English translation of the Hebrew "Yahweh," which is the personal name of God used in the Old Testament. In some places it has been difficult for me to decide whether to use "God" or "Lord," because they both give revelation and both inspire prophetic messages. To use only "God" or only "Lord" is to exclude one, but to use "God or the Lord" seems too wordy. By using "Lord" many times in this book, I have tried to recognize the Lord Jesus as head of the Church, and recognize the fact that he does inspire prophecy. I am certainly not trying to dishonor God in any fashion, but recognize that "…He who does not honor the Son does not honor the Father, who sent him" (John 5:23b).

1. Prophecy is speaking, writing, or otherwise communicating a message from God to a person or persons. When God or the Lord Jesus Christ gives a message to a person to deliver to an individual or group, and he delivers that message, it is prophecy. Although prophecy is usually spoken, it may also be delivered by writing it out and then delivering the written message, or it may be given another way, such as sign language. The point is, when a message from God or the Lord Jesus is delivered from one person to another, that is prophecy. When the message comes to the one who is charged with delivering it, it is "revelation" to that person.[2] It becomes prophecy when it is communicated to others.

Because it is the communication of a message, prophecy can occur in many outward forms as an action or utterance. It is an outward expression of the inner move of the spirit of God. When God communicates a message through people, we describe what the people do as "prophetic." For example, when God inspires a dancer to dance such that a message from God is communicated to His people, that is called "prophetic dancing." If a painter paints a picture as God directs or inspires, and that picture communicates a message from God's heart, that would be "prophetic." It is sometimes the case that prophets are asked to act out the prophetic message. God commanded Hosea to marry a prostitute to communicate how He felt being "married" to Israel (Hosea 1:2). God commanded Jeremiah to put a yoke on his neck and wear it to communicate that Judah should not rebel against Babylon, but come under their yoke (Jer. 27:1-12). Agabus bound his own hands and feet to illustrate that Paul would be bound when he got to Jerusalem (Acts 21:10 and 11).

To fully understand prophetic action, it is important to realize that "messages" from God can be very subtle, sometimes relating only His love for us, or His greatness. For example, when God inspires a dancer or a painter, there may not be a specific directional message from the Lord that the audience is supposed to understand and act on, although there certainly could be. The message might be more along the lines of God communicating His glory to us.

---

2. For an explanation of "revelation," see Appendix D: "Revelation: What It Is and How It Is Received."

2. Prophecy is communicating a message that has been received by revelation. Most revelation is for the person who receives it, and is not intended to be communicated to others. For example, God told Abraham to leave Mesopotamia and go to another land (Gen. 12:1). That revelation was from God to Abraham, but was not a message that He wanted Abraham to deliver to others, so it was not prophecy. When God spoke to Moses from the burning bush, it was revelation to Moses but not prophecy because it was not a message that Moses was to deliver to the Israelites (Exod. 3:4ff). God told Elijah to go hide by the brook and allow the ravens to feed him (1 Kings 17:2-6). This information was revelation to Elijah but was never prophecy because it was not intended to be communicated as a message to others. However, when God gives someone revelation He wants communicated to others, and that person communicates the revelation, it becomes prophecy.

3. Prophecy is communicating a revelation given either at an earlier time or right at the moment the person is speaking, or it can be a combination of the two. Prophecy falls into two basic categories. The first and most common is inspirational and non-cognitive, which we call "inspirational prophecy." The second is cognitive and deliberate. From God's perspective, prophecy is simply part of a person's walk with God, and therefore the Bible does not divide it into these two categories. However, to better understand prophecy and how it works, it is helpful to see the two basic categories into which it falls.

In inspirational prophecy, the person giving the prophecy does not know the prophetic message ahead of time. The Lord gives the words to him as he speaks. This type of prophecy is inspirational, non-cognitive, spontaneous, and "in the moment." In contrast to inspirational prophecy, there are times when God gives a message to someone long before it is ever spoken. The message may come weeks, days, hours, or minutes before it is spoken as prophecy. It is up to the one who received the message from God to hold it in his mind until the time it is delivered. In contrast to inspirational prophecy, this kind of prophecy is very deliberate. Both kinds of prophecy are in the Bible, and most people who have given corporate and personal prophecy for several years or more will testify to having had messages from God both ahead of time and in the moment.

The Bible has some clear examples of inspirational prophecy. 1 Kings 13:21 and 22 is a prophecy by an old prophet to a young one who had been tricked into disobeying the LORD. God energized holy spirit inside the old prophet, and he spoke a prophecy without any forethought. He was simply energized by God and spoke out, with God giving the message as he spoke. In 2 Chronicles 15:1-7, the spirit of God came upon Azariah and he gave an inspirational and encouraging prophecy to Asa and the people of Judah. In 2 Chronicles 20:14-17, the spirit of God energized Jahaziel and he spoke an inspired prophecy to Jehoshaphat and the people of Judah. In 2 Chronicles 24:20, the spirit of God energized Zechariah and he gave an inspired word of reproof to the people of Judah for their sin. In Acts 4:10-12, Peter gave an inspired message to the rulers of Israel. In Acts 13:8-11, the Apostle Paul gave an inspired word to Elymas. These are examples of the people prophesying as they are inspired and energized by God. As they stepped out in faith and began to speak, God gave them the words.

Just as there are clear examples of inspirational prophecy, there are many examples of God giving the person the message by revelation ahead of time. An excellent one is when God told Nathan to go tell David that he would not be the one to build the Temple (2 Sam. 7:4-17).

4. Prophecy is not speaking *about* information that has been received by revelation. There are times when prophecy is very easy to identify, and there are times when a message is harder to identify as prophecy per se. When God or the Lord Jesus gives someone a message for another person, and that message is spoken, that is prophecy. However, just talking about the revelation one has received is not prophecy. One of the boundaries of prophecy that can be difficult to pin down is when someone is speaking about what he has received from the Lord by revelation, but what he is saying is more along the lines of sharing information than delivering a message. For example, in 1 Kings 18:22-24, Elijah instructed the people how to prove whether Yahweh or Baal was the true God by seeing which of the two would answer by fire.[3] The trial was God's design (1 Kings 18:36). Nevertheless, what Elijah said to the people was not prophecy because it was not a "message" for them, it was simply his letting them know what God had communicated to him by revelation. Another example is when God told Moses what to do in Egypt, and then Moses told it to Aaron (Exod. 4:28). Even though Moses told Aaron the information he had received by revelation, that kind of communication is not prophecy.

Prophecy as a Manifestation of Holy Spirit

Some prophecy is a manifestation of the gift of holy spirit, and some prophecy is not. Prophecy as a manifestation of the gift of holy spirit occurs when God, or the Lord Jesus, gives a revelation message to an individual by way of the holy spirit sealed inside him, which becomes prophecy when it is communicated to others. Every Christian has the gift of holy spirit sealed within him,[4] which he received when he accepted

---

3. "Yahweh" is the personal name of God. It first occurs in Genesis 2:4 and then more than 6,000 times in the Old Testament. It is translated "Jehovah" in some versions, but in most versions it is translated "Lord." The word "lord" is a general title for any lord, master, owner, or overseer. In contrast, "Yahweh" is God's personal name; it is not a title or general term. Always translating "Yahweh" as "Lord" is very much like always calling someone "Sir" or "Mister," and never using his real name. In the contest between Yahweh and Baal, this distinction becomes very important, because in Hebrew, "Baal" is both the name of a specific pagan god and a general title meaning "lord, owner, husband, ruler." Translating "Yahweh" as "Lord" in this context can reduce the contest to simply which "lord" will be the one worshipped by Israel.

4. "The Holy Spirit" (capital "H," capital "S") refers to God. At the time a person becomes saved, he is given God's divine nature (2 Pet. 1:4). Because God is holy (Isa. 6:3), and God is spirit (John 4:24), His nature is "holy spirit." Throughout Christian history, much confusion has been caused by not understanding the difference between the Holy Spirit (God, the Giver) and holy spirit (the gift, the divine nature). The gift of holy spirit inside an individual cannot be detected by the five senses. However, it can be "manifested," brought to light. Prophecy is one of the nine manifestations listed in 1 Corinthians 12. For more on the difference between the Holy Spirit and holy spirit, see our book by Mark Graeser, John Lynn, John Schoenheit, "Chapter One: It's Greek to

Christ and was "born again" (Rom. 10:9 and 10; Eph. 1:13).[5] Most prophecy spoken by Christians comes from God via the holy spirit inside them and, because of that, one of the nine manifestations of the gift of holy spirit is "prophecy" (1 Cor. 12:7 and 10).

Although the manifestation of prophecy is by far the most common form of prophecy, it is important to realize that prophecy does not have to be a manifestation of holy spirit. Remember, prophecy is communicating a message that is given to someone by revelation. If that revelation, for example, comes directly from the Lord Jesus Christ, i.e., if the Lord Jesus were to personally appear to an individual and give him a message to deliver, when that message was delivered, it would be prophecy. However, it would not be the "manifestation" of prophecy because the Lord did not speak to the individual via the gift of holy spirit inside him, but instead appeared personally. Similarly, if an angel were to appear to someone and give him a message for someone else, when the message was delivered it would be prophecy, but it would not be the manifestation of prophecy because the holy spirit inside the believer was not energized.

Why is There Prophecy?

The origin of prophecy is the loving heart of a Father God. God loves His people and wants to have a relationship with them. He wants us to walk and talk with Him and live blessed lives. Prophecy demonstrates

---

me (Why we use both Holy Spirit and holy spirit)" and "Chapter Two: The Giver and the Gift," *The Gift of Holy Spirit: The Power To Be Like Christ* (Christian Educational Services, Indianapolis, IN, 2006).

5. People have argued for centuries about what makes someone a "Christian." Biblically, a Christian is one who has obeyed Romans 10:9. He has confessed Jesus as his Lord and has believed that God raised him from the dead. At that time God places the fullness of holy spirit, His divine nature, in the person, and he becomes a Christian. Going to church, doing good deeds, being immersed in water, believing in God, etc., are all good works, but they do not make one a Christian because they do not result in his having the fullness of holy spirit sealed inside him. A Christian has holy spirit on the inside, and thus can hear from God. For more information, see our booklet *Becoming a Christian: Why? What? How?* by Christian Educational Services, which can be read in its entirety on www.TruthOrTradition.com TOPIC: Recommended Reading.

God's love for us in a very tangible way. Furthermore, God wants healthy relationships between people in the Body of Christ and in the world, and prophecy helps build such relationships.

As any loving Father would speak to his children, God speaks by prophecy both to His children and to other people. He gives them words of blessing, encouragement, comfort, and hope; He directs us in the way we should go; He says things that build our faith and gives us confidence in His presence and love. He also exhorts us when we need to "get up and get going," and He gives us warnings when we are straying or when something is coming in the future that we cannot foresee. God also knows that prophecy builds relationships in the family of God. He gives messages that allow us to help each other in meaningful and beneficial ways.

When prophecy is not present in the Church, many blessings are missed. Proverbs 29:18a says that when there is no revelation from God, the people are "let alone."[6] Good parents know that letting children alone is a formula for disaster. Proverbs 29:15b says, "...a child left to himself disgraces his mother." It is never God's heart to leave us alone. He wants to communicate His love and bless us. Prophecy is a major way that God speaks to

> The origin of prophecy is the loving heart of a Father God.

us to bless us and build our relationship with Him, which then helps us be more Christ-like in our relationship with other people.

---

6. The NASB translation of Proverbs 29:18a says, "Where there is no vision, [i.e., no revelation from God], the people are unrestrained...." The phrase "are unrestrained" does not quite communicate the full meaning in this context. The Hebrew word means, "let go, let alone" (*Brown-Driver-Briggs Hebrew And English Lexicon*). It is used of "uncovering" someone or something by taking off clothing; making naked; and "letting go" of wise counsel by refusing or ignoring it. When people walk without God to the end that there is not prophetic vision, they are, in effect, "let go" by God. At that point, of course, many of them follow their fleshly desires and act in an unrestrained fashion. However, some "perish" (KJV), and of course, without God's provision and covering, they are all "naked" (YLT) and exposed to the tricks and traps of the Adversary.

The fact that relationship with God is the underlying theme of prophecy helps explain why He gives prophetic information in so many ways. While it is certainly true that the majority of prophecies can be taken at face value and understood by the most unlearned believer, anyone who has dealt with prophecy for a period of years has encountered prophetic messages that are unclear, as perhaps in a dream or vision.

If God's purpose in prophecy were only to communicate a message, He would speak clearly and simply all the time, which He is certainly capable of doing. But giving us information is not all that God wants. God is not just a dispenser of information. The ultimate purpose of His communication is to establish loving relationships with us. By occasionally speaking in ways that are not immediately clear, God pushes us into a deeper relationship with Him. He compels us to go to Him over and over asking Him for more, while also searching our hearts about the message. We ask ourselves, "Would it be clearer if I were closer to Him? Or more godly? Or hadn't lost my temper and cussed yesterday?" We ask Him, "God, what did you mean? Please, say it again. Say it clearer." Sometimes we ask, then find ourselves having to pray and ask again, then perhaps even fasting and praying and asking again. We examine our lives, hearts, and relationships, and ask again. Meanwhile we know that God is always beckoning, and is always there, loving us and giving us help and hope.

> God communicates many "matters" in ways that take diligent searching to discover their full meaning.

Because everyone who deals with prophecy will eventually experience it being unclear, it is important to understand that God purposely communicates it that way. This point is made several times in Scripture. In Numbers, God says He communicates in "riddles."

Numbers 12:5-8a

(5) Then the LORD came down in a pillar of cloud; he stood at the entrance to the Tent and summoned Aaron and Miriam. When both of them stepped forward,

(6) he said, "Listen to my words: "When a prophet of the LORD is among you, I reveal myself to him in visions, I speak to him in dreams.

(7) But this is not true of my servant Moses; he is faithful in all my house.

(8a) With him I speak face to face, clearly and not in riddles; he sees the form of the LORD…

Seasoned prophets can recount many times when God has communicated to them in "riddles." Proverbs also says that God sometimes communicates in obscure messages:

Proverbs 25:2
It is the glory of God to conceal a matter; to search out a matter is the glory of kings.

God communicates many "matters" in ways that take diligent searching to discover their full meaning.

Like his Father, Jesus often spoke in ways his audience did not understand. For example, he spoke in parables to the crowds, knowing they did not understand what he was communicating. After Jesus told the parable of the sower and the seed, the disciples realized the audience did not understand it, and asked Jesus why he spoke in parables.

Matthew 13:10 and 11
(10) The disciples came to him and asked, "Why do you speak to the people in parables?"

(11) He replied, "The knowledge of the secrets of the kingdom of heaven has been given to you, but not to them.

Many more scriptures show that God and Jesus communicate in ways that require thought, reflection, and diligent searching, but the point is that God has a reason for communicating as He does. He wants people to have a relationship with Him and with each other, and occasionally communicating obscurely helps accomplish that purpose. He also wants His people to value each other and work together. When an unclear prophetic word is given, it often occurs that people work together to pray and seek its meaning.

The purpose of prophecy is clearly revealed in prophecy. The prophecies in the Bible and those given today reveal the heart of God. God expresses His love and thanksgiving to His children. He speaks words that edify and comfort us. He exhorts us to more and more godliness in our walk with Him, and more and more love and commitment toward other people. He directs us in our lives so we can be blessed, and can clearly see how loving and caring He is, and then thank and love Him in return. As God's love pours out to us via His prophetic word, then we, receiving that word and the love that is behind it, are then able to love God and one another to a greater degree, just as Scripture says, "We love because he first loved us" (1 John 4:19).

Is Prophecy Always About the Future?

Prophecy can be about the past, present, or future. Sometimes we need to be reminded of a past event so we can think clearly about the situation we are in and how we are behaving. At other times we need to hear from God about the present situation so that we can know what is happening from His point of view, and know what we should do. Prophecy about the future is the most well known aspect of prophecy, and the Bible contains dozens and dozens of examples.

A good example of God giving a prophecy about past events to get the Israelites to think clearly about their situation occurs in Judges.

Judges 6:7-10
(7) When the Israelites cried to the LORD because of Midian, (8) he sent them a prophet, who said, "This is what the LORD, the God of Israel, says: I brought you up out of Egypt, out of the land of slavery.
(9) I snatched you from the power of Egypt and from the hand of all your oppressors. I drove them from before you and gave you their land.
(10) I said to you, 'I am the LORD your God; do not worship the

gods of the Amorites, in whose land you live.' But you have not listened to me."

The information in this prophecy is about the past, to remind the Israelites how good God had been to them. It contains nothing about the future. Also, it has no instructions telling the people what to do—how they were to behave was obvious from the Mosaic Law, so it was not necessary for God to say anything.

Another reason God uses the past in prophecy is so that we recognize that He knows us and has been involved with our lives. Hearing from God through prophecy establishes a connection and confidence between Him and us that may not have been there before. Jesus used this to good effect with the Samaritan woman he met at Jacob's well when he told her that she had had five husbands (John 4:18). She immediately realized he was a prophet, and was soon connected with him to such a degree that she went into town and said to others, "Come, see a man who told me everything I ever did…" (John 4:29a). Of course, Jesus had not told her "everything" she ever did, but his prophetic word to her produced a heart connection so strong that she felt like he knew her intimately. Many people who have suffered in life are very comforted when they hear prophetic words showing conclusively that the Lord has been with them through their trials, and understands what they have been through.

> Prophecy can be about the past, present, or future.

Prophecy also addresses present situations, and there are many reasons why, but the most prevalent is to tell people what to do or not to do. God cares very much for His people, and He wants to participate in their lives and help them succeed. Because of that, many prophecies deal with current situations. Deborah told Barak to take 10,000 men and go to Mount Tabor (Judg. 4:6). Samuel told Saul that people will tell him that his donkeys have been found and his father has started to worry about him (1 Sam. 10:2). Gad told David not to remain where he was but to go into Judah (1 Sam. 22:5). Elisha told Naaman the Syrian wash in the Jordan seven times to be cleansed from leprosy (2 Kings 5:10). An unnamed prophet, at the direction of Elisha, declared that Jehu was anointed king and that he was to destroy the house of Ahab (2 Kings 9:6 and 7).

Prophecy can also be about what is coming in the future. For example, there are many prophecies in the Old Testament about the coming Messiah. Often the Lord will tell us what is coming so we can prepare for it. For example, in Acts 11:28, the prophet Agabus warned the Church that there was going to be a famine. The church responded by preparing for it, and sent help to those who were hardest hit (Acts 11:29 and 30). Often, prophecy is a combination of past, present, and future. For example, the prophecy of Nathan to David after David said he wanted to build a Temple for God contained all three elements (2 Sam. 7:4-16).

When Christians operate the manifestation of prophecy and give a message to a person, Scripture notes that, "…the secrets of his heart will be laid bare…" (1 Cor. 14:25a). The message does not have to be about the person's future. God is working to establish a personal relationship with the individual, and His revealing the secrets of his heart helps to do exactly that.

The Nature of the Prophetic Message

Biblical prophecy is often misunderstood in the world today. Most people think of prophecy as God making known His unchanging purposes through a prophet. In other words, God speaks, then what He says comes to pass at some later date. Although that certainly is one aspect of prophecy, it is by no means all there is to prophecy. We have seen that the reason God gives words of prophecy is that He loves us and wants a relationship with us. When we understand that, we are in a position to understand more about the nature of the prophetic message.

We have just seen above that prophecy can be about the past, present, or future. A large part of God's prophetic word is His working to build relationships with His people: communicating His love, fighting for their love, trying to get them to turn from evil, drawing them to Him by His care and kindness. This fact becomes very clear when we consider the entire Bible as prophecy, which, of course, it is. Prophecy is not "in" the

Bible, **it is the Bible**. The entire Bible is a message from God brought to us through His spokesmen. How many verses of Scripture, brought to us by God's messengers such as Moses, Samuel, Isaiah, Paul, Peter, etc., express God's love? How many express His forgiveness and mercy? How many exhort us to righteousness? Hundreds? Thousands? Certainly a lot.

Once we consider that the Bible **is** prophecy, we are in a position to ask, "What is the nature of the prophetic message?", and properly answer it. Prophecy spoken today can have as many purposes as the prophetic message that makes up the Bible. Obviously, one of the things God does in prophecy is foretell the future so that when it comes to pass we know He is God (Isa. 41:21-24,[7] 42:9, 44:7, 45:21, 48:3-5). However, that is only a very small part of the wide range of prophetic messages.

It is important to understand the wide range of prophecy because when a person receives a prophetic message, it may contain nothing about the future. It may simply be an expression of God's love and care for the person. An uneducated person might think, "That was not a real prophecy," based on his belief that a prophecy should have something about his future. However, receiving a message about God's love can be prophecy, and should never be discounted. Of course, given the scope of subjects that prophecy could cover, a person might receive blessings, direction, warning, or any number of things about his life.

Prophecy in the Bible, and the prophecy spoken by the individuals in the Church who have the specific ministry of a prophet, can cover any subject God wants to. However, when a Christian who is not a prophet gives a prophecy that is a manifestation of prophecy, the prophetic

---

7. These verses in Isaiah 41 make the point that idols cannot tell the future. God is contrasting these idols, which cannot tell the future, with Himself, who can, and shows Himself to be the true God by doing so. The fact that idols cannot tell the future exposes them as false gods. Scripture says we should know God is God because He accurately foretells what is coming in the future, which of course, He does. This one clear evidence for God's existence exposes the folly of those people who refuse to believe in God.

message will almost always fall into one of the following three categories: edification, exhortation, or comfort (1 Cor. 14:3-KJV).[8]

Is All Prophecy From God?

Both the true God and the Devil give prophecy. True prophecy is a message from the true God, and false prophecy is a message from the false god, who is the Devil. The Devil always works to thwart what God is doing. The Devil counterfeits God's prophetic message to further his devilish purposes, to defame God, and to procure worship for himself. Because prophecy is important to God and His work, the Devil works hard to denounce it and promote his own means of speaking from the spirit world. If there is one thing that the existence of the Devil's counterfeit shows, it is that **there is a genuine!** Sadly, some people are so aware of the counterfeit, or afraid of it, that they will not seek the genuine for fear of operating the counterfeit. We believe it is a huge mistake not to seek the genuine manifestation of prophecy. It is very valuable to the Lord and to the Church, which is why there is prophecy in the first place.

True Prophecy	False Prophecy
Lord Jesus	Demon
↓	↓
Prophet	Psychic
↓	↓
Person	Person

There are many ways that information from the Devil and his evil kingdom come into our world. Usually a demon that the Bible calls a "spirit of divination" (Acts 16:16-KJV) enters a person and gives him information.[9] In Jeremiah, God said that "...The prophets prophesied by

---

8. These words are defined in the Glossary, and more will be said about them later.

9. The NIV says the slave woman had "...a spirit by which she predicted the future...." Although this was true, a spirit of divination can give all sorts of detailed information about people, not just their future. Usually, it is this detailed information that "hooks" people into following the advice of the demon. The actual demon in Acts 16 was "a

Baal…" (Jer. 2:8) meaning that the prophets were bringing a word from a demonic source. False information comes directly or indirectly. An example of directly getting satanic information is when a false prophet, medium, or psychic hears directly from a demon (although they usually think it is from God or a "good spirit"). Examples of indirectly receiving satanic information include divining with such things as tarot cards, tea leaves, Ouija Boards, dice, knucklebones, crystal balls, etc. In those cases, a demon influences the environment to produce the satanically inspired result.

It is important to understand that much of the information that comes from satanic sources is true. If it were not, even unbelievers would very quickly dismiss it as false or unhelpful. The Devil is a crafty fisherman, and as a fisherman hides a hook in a worm, he hides lies and deceit in the midst of truth. He gets a person to the point that he trusts what the false prophet or psychic says, and then gives a piece of false information that will turn him away from God, truth, or deceive him in some other way that will eventually lead to his ruin. A Christian should never seek information from a demonic source. It is a sin against God (Deut. 18:12) and will eventually end up in his ruin. The wise Christian knows the Devil's tactics and is not fooled by the truth that a psychic, medium, etc., learns from the spirit world. Sooner or later, the hook will be revealed.

The Adversary's counterfeit prophecies have kept many Christians away from prophecy altogether. From God's perspective, this is tragic. God gave prophecy to be a great blessing and, used properly, it can accomplish many wonderful things. The way to avoid the counterfeit is by knowing how and why both the genuine and the counterfeit work.

The best way for a Christian to avoid receiving counterfeit prophecy is to stay away from obvious counterfeits (like psychic hotlines) and make wise choices about the people from whom to receive a prophecy. Since demons almost always work to disrupt a godly lifestyle, one of

---

spirit of Python" (Greek text), the Python spirit being the symbol of Apollo, and the spirit inhabiting the Oracle at Delphi in Ancient Greece.

the wisest choices a person can make is to not receive a prophecy from someone who has an ungodly lifestyle (and remember, some "religious" people are ungodly). They could be right on the money with what they say, but then again, they may be being led by a demon, and their words may not be pure. Also, it is always good for a person to get some godly counselors to listen to any prophecy he receives.

One way that the spirit of divination gains access to an individual is by his asking for information he has no business knowing, or does not need to know. A spirit of divination will gladly give information that God will not give. When King Saul sought information from God, and He would not answer, a demon was more than happy to accommodate Saul through the medium (technically, "necromancer") who lived at Endor (1 Sam. 28). It is very important to know the written Word and have a feel for the heart of God. Asking for details about someone's life that you have no business knowing can invite a demon into your mind. For example, when God forgives someone, He forgets his sin. Do not ask God any details about past sins that have been confessed. He will not reveal anything, but a demon will.

> The best way for a Christian to avoid receiving counterfeit prophecy is to stay away from obvious counterfeits (like psychic hotlines) and make wise choices about the people from whom to receive a prophecy.

Having honest and godly motivation for the things one does is a great key to keeping demons out. If a person is motivated by fear of failure or of doing something that is not God's will, he will be tempted to ask God about every little thing and be afraid to move forward until he gets an answer. God gives each person the ability to think and make decisions, and He expects us to use what He gave us. Both God and the Lord Jesus Christ want an intimate relationship with each Christian, and want us to talk to them and seek them out each and every day. However, the wise Christian knows that if his gas tank is on "E," although he may ask God if he should stop and get gas now or later, God may not answer that, expecting him to use wisdom and make the choice himself. Demanding that God give an answer for things that are knowable in the senses world, and refusing to act until He answers is not wise, and can invite a demon into your life. The demon will be more than happy to gratify your desire to feel directed by God.

God will not answer a request to help someone participate successfully in ungodly activities. Someone may ask God, "Tell me what house on this block has an open door and no one inside so I can get some money and pay my bills," but He will not answer. If a person keeps asking for spiritual guidance to accomplish ungodly goals, a demon may enter into his life that will help him accomplish what he wants to do. James 4:3 says that people who ask God with wrong motives do not get what they are asking from God, and that is true. They might, however, get it from a demon. Christians need to check their motives with the written Word and get wise counsel from other mature Christians if they are in doubt about whether or not God will answer a certain request.

CHAPTER TWO
The Conditional Nature of Prophecy

Much Prophecy is Conditional

We have seen in the previous chapter that prophecy is giving a message from God or the Lord Jesus to another person or persons, and that the main reason for prophecy is God's love for us. God wants a relationship with us, and He wants to show His love for us and desires us to love Him.

We now need to examine an aspect of prophecy that is very important, and not well understood by most Christians: when a prophecy is spoken to people about them personally, it is almost always conditional in nature. The fulfillment of the prophecy often depends on the attitude and actions of the one to whom the prophecy is given. This is different from the generally accepted teaching that when God declares something, it is "set in stone," and will absolutely come to pass. If you are one who has believed that a true prophet of God is defined by the fact that his prophecies always come to pass, you should carefully read this chapter, and also Appendix B, "False Prophets and False Prophecies."

Certainly there are prophecies from God that are "set in stone" and will come to pass exactly as God spoke them, but not all prophecies are that way. Prophecies spoken to individuals or groups about what will happen to them in the future are usually conditional upon the actions and attitudes of the people addressed. God gave us free will, and He responds to the free will decisions we make. What makes the prophecy conditional is there is an unspoken "if" in the prophecy. In other words, the prophecy has a condition in it.

Another way to look at the conditional nature of prophecy is to remember that prophecy is an expression of God's love for people, and that many times in prophecy God is calling us to greater things, rather than just announcing what will happen in the future, as if He would then gloat when it happened. Take the prophecy Jonah gave to the people of Nineveh: "…Forty more days and Nineveh will be overturned."

(Jon. 3:4b). Anyone reading the book of Jonah sees that Jonah's prophecy did not come to pass. Nevertheless, Jonah was a true prophet. Furthermore, had the prophecy been fulfilled as spoken without being conditional, then what would have been the point? To tell thousands of people they were going to die in 40 days? No, there is another explanation.

The prophecy of Jonah, and other prophecies to people, often have an unspoken "if" clause. When the "if" is expressed, the prophecy looks like this: "Forty more days and Nineveh will be overturned if you do not change." God is expressing His love via a prophecy that calls people to greater things. The prophecy gives people a chance to rise up and walk in a godly fashion before Him. The people of Nineveh did, and therefore God's prophecy was not fulfilled. Of course, sometimes a prophecy of good is spoken, but the people turn to evil. Those prophecies are also conditional, and the good that was foretold often does not come to pass.

There are many times when the "if" of revelation or prophecy is clearly spoken.[1] For example, in Genesis 20, Abimelech of Gerar had taken Abraham's wife Sarah to be his wife. He did this not knowing that Sarah was married to Abraham, because Abraham had told him Sarah was his "sister." God said to Abimelech: "Now return the man's wife, for he is a prophet, and he will pray for you and you will live. But **if** you do not return her, you may be sure that you and all yours will die" (Gen. 20:7). In this case, God said "if" you do not return her you will die, but how would the revelation have looked were there no "if"? God would have just announced that Abimelech would die because he had taken another man's wife, and then He would have changed the revelation if Abimelech repented and returned Sarah to Abraham. God can change a revelation or a prophecy, and in this chapter we will see many examples of Him doing so when the people who received the prophecy changed their behavior.

There are two primary reasons why it is important to know that prophecy is so often conditional. The first is to build and maintain faith in God and His prophets. People who do not realize that prophecy is conditional may

---

1. A few examples are: Deuteronomy 15:4-6, 28:1-9; 1 Samuel 7:3, 12:25; 1 Kings 3:14, 6:12, 11:38; Isaiah 1:18-20; Jeremiah 12:14-17.

have their faith shaken if a particular prophecy does not come to pass or if they see a prophecy in the Bible that did not come to pass. For example, a person operating under the premise that true prophecy must come to pass as spoken is forced to say that Jonah was a false prophet. But we know that Jonah was a true prophet of God. If a particular prophecy is not fulfilled, we should examine the prophecy and the situation to see if the reason that it was not fulfilled had to do with a shift in the situation.

The second reason it is important to know that prophecy can be conditional is that people need to know that their behavior can affect whether or not a prophecy comes to pass. A Christian who is walking with the Lord needs to continue in faith, prayer, and an obedient lifestyle. On the other hand, a disobedient person who receives an undesirable prophecy can repent, in which case the prophecy that he had received may either not be fulfilled (just as Jonah's prophecy to the Ninevites was not), or changed (as we will see in Hezekiah's case).

Jeremiah Sets Forth the Conditional Nature of Prophecy

In the book of Jeremiah, God reveals the conditional nature of prophecy, and He compared His working with people with a potter working with clay. Please read the following section of Jeremiah carefully, because Christians have misunderstood it for centuries.

Jeremiah 18:1-11
(1) This is the word that came to Jeremiah from the LORD:
(2) "Go down to the potter's house, and there I will give you my message."
(3) So I went down to the potter's house, and I saw him working at the wheel.
(4) But the pot he was shaping from the clay was marred in his hands; so the potter formed it into another pot, shaping it as seemed best to him.
(5) Then the word of the LORD came to me:
(6) "O house of Israel, can I not do with you as this potter does?" declares the LORD. "Like clay in the hand of the potter, so are you

in my hand, O house of Israel.

(7) If at any time I announce that a nation or kingdom is to be uprooted, torn down and destroyed,

(8) and if that nation I warned repents of its evil, then I will relent and not inflict on it the disaster I had planned.

(9) And if at another time I announce that a nation or kingdom is to be built up and planted,

(10) and if it does evil in my sight and does not obey me, then I will reconsider the good I had intended to do for it.

(11) "Now therefore say to the people of Judah and those living in Jerusalem, 'This is what the LORD says: Look! I am preparing a disaster for you and devising a plan against you. So turn from your evil ways, each one of you, and reform your ways and your actions."

Many people think that the lesson the potter and the clay teaches is that God can do anything He wants to with people. However, that is not the case. In fact, the lesson is actually the opposite. The potter knew what he wanted to make from the clay, but when he tried to make it, it was "marred" in his hand (v. 4). The clay was uncooperative, and would not take the shape the potter had in mind. The potter did not mar the clay, it was marred in itself. This is a common occurrence in pottery, as every experienced potter knows.

In order for the potter to form his idea out of clay, the lump of clay must cooperate. It is not unusual for a potter to try to make a vase or pot and have the clay seem not to want to form into that shape. In that case the potter simply does what the potter in Jeremiah did thousands of years ago: he collapses the pot and starts over, often with a new idea.

People and clay are a lot alike, and God, the ultimate potter, works with us like a potter does with clay. God has an idea for our lives, but often we are uncooperative, and will not take the shape He desires for us. What does God do? He does His best to work with our free will and make something different out of our lives. The reason God had Jeremiah go to the potter's house was to teach Jeremiah that the way God works with people depends on what the people are willing to do.

After the verses about the potter and clay, verses 7-10 explain the way God works with people as they exercise their free will. In verse seven, God gives a prophetic message that a kingdom is to be torn down. If prophecy were inflexible and final as stated, then that would happen: the fate of the nation would be sealed. But wait! In verse eight God says that if, in response to the prophecy, the nation repents and turns from evil, then He will not follow through with what He planned to do. Similarly, in verse nine, God gives a prophecy that a nation would be built up and "planted," i.e., established. However, if the nation becomes evil and disobedient, like a piece of clay that will simply not take the proper shape, then God cannot follow through with the good He had prophesied about that nation, but has to change His plans. After all, God cannot force people to be obedient. Thus is it clear that whether or not a prophecy is fulfilled depends on the people to whom it is given.

> People and clay are a lot alike, and God, the ultimate potter, works with us like a potter does with clay.

The lesson of the potter is applied to Judah and Jerusalem in verse eleven. In Jeremiah's time, God's prophets had been giving prophecies that Jerusalem would be destroyed. There are many examples in Jeremiah alone, but one will suffice.

Jeremiah 4:5-7
(5) "Announce in Judah and proclaim in Jerusalem and say: 'Sound the trumpet throughout the land!' Cry aloud and say: 'Gather together! Let us flee to the fortified cities!'
(6) Raise the signal to go to Zion! Flee for safety without delay! For I am bringing disaster from the north [i.e., from Babylon], even terrible destruction."
(7) A lion has come out of his lair; a destroyer of nations has set out. He has left his place to lay waste your land. Your towns will lie in ruins without inhabitant.

Even though God had prophesied that Judah would be destroyed for her sin, it is clear from the potter example in Jeremiah 18 that God, in His amazing grace, was telling Judah that if they repented they would not be destroyed after all. Sadly, Judah did not repent or change her evil ways. In an astounding show of stubbornness, the Judeans decided to continue in their ungodly ways. They said:

Jeremiah 18:12b
"...It's no use. We will continue with our own plans; each of us will follow the stubbornness of his evil heart."

We know from both the Bible and secular history that Judah did not repent, and that they were destroyed by Babylon "from the north," just as God had said.

The important thing for us to learn in this study is that if Judah had repented, God would have relented and saved the country, and His prophecies of their destruction would not have come to pass. Thus, in the record in Jeremiah 18, God specifically shows us two types of prophecies that may be conditional: prophecies that foretell disaster, and prophecies that promise blessings. These prophecies are spoken to people, and are usually conditional.

Prophecies That Changed

We are now going to examine a number of prophecies in the Bible that were spoken but not fulfilled. These examples clearly reveal the conditional nature of prophecy, and help us see that God is doing much more than just predicting the future when He gives a prophecy. He is calling people to Himself and working to build the fellowship between God and man. This section is long because the information is new and challenging to most people, and therefore many examples are given to establish the truth of the point. If you understand the concept, and do not want to read all the examples, skip down to the next section, "Prophecies That Did Not Change."

Saul's kingship. God gave Samuel the revelation that Saul would be king over Israel (1 Sam. 9:17). That revelation became prophecy when Samuel spoke it to Saul (1 Sam. 10:1). The implied part of the prophecy is that both Saul and his descendants would reign over Israel. There would have been no reason for the prophet to speak that, because that was simply the way kingdoms work: after the king dies, a descendant becomes king. Yet Saul disobeyed the word of God, and Samuel delivered a prophecy that modified the original prophecy, stating that Saul's kingdom would not endure. The original prophecy was conditional upon Saul's obedience to God.

1 Samuel 13:13 and 14

(13) "You [Saul] acted foolishly," Samuel said. "You have not kept the command the LORD your God gave you; if you had, he would have established your kingdom over Israel for all time.
(14) But now your kingdom will not endure; the LORD has sought out a man after his own heart and appointed him leader of his people, because you have not kept the LORD's command."

Upon receiving the prophecy that his kingdom would not endure, one would think that Saul would have repented in dust and ashes and prayed fervently to have God's blessing restored. Not so. Saul continued to sin, and Samuel confronted him again.

1 Samuel 15:23, 26-28

(23) "For rebellion is like the sin of divination, and arrogance like the evil of idolatry. Because you have rejected the word of the LORD, he has rejected you as king."
(26) But Samuel said to him [Saul], "I will not go back with you. You have rejected the word of the LORD, and the LORD has rejected you as king over Israel!"
(27) As Samuel turned to leave, Saul caught hold of the hem of his robe, and it tore.
(28) Samuel said to him, "The LORD has torn the kingdom of Israel from you today and has given it to one of your neighbors—to one

better than you."

Notice that in verse 28 God had torn the kingdom from Saul "today." This is very important. God is longsuffering. He puts up with a lot of disobedience on the part of His servants, but He has His limits. Saul had disobeyed before, often grievously. But this disobedience regarding the Amalekites was the last straw. God removed His holy spirit from Saul, who then became afflicted by demons (1 Sam. 16:14). Saul still acted as king, but without God's blessing, while David won the hearts of the people. Even Jonathan, the crown prince and next in line to be king, realized that the kingdom had passed from Saul, and said to David, "…You will be king over Israel…" (1 Sam. 23:17).

The peace in David's lifetime. David had done many wonderful things for God, and so He sent Nathan the prophet with the following message for David: "…I will also give you rest from all your enemies…" (2 Sam. 7:11). There is no doubt that Nathan was a true prophet of God, and if the paradigm of most Christians is right—that a prophecy once spoken will absolutely come to pass, then David would have had rest from his enemies for the rest of his life. However, we know that prophecy spoken to people is often conditional upon what they do after they receive it, and that was the case with David. He did not continue steadfastly in the ways of God. After David committed adultery with Bathsheba and had Uriah murdered, God changed His prophecy to David. He sent Nathan again, but with a different message: "Now, therefore, the sword will never depart from your house…" (2 Sam. 12:10a).

The phrase, "Now, therefore" alerts us to the fact that there has been a change in the prophetic message, and we see that played out through the rest of David's life. He had to fight his own son, Absalom, to keep the throne, squash the rebellion of Sheba the Benjamite (2 Sam. 20), and battle the Philistines (2 Sam. 21:15).

Solomon's kingdom. Another good example of the conditional nature of prophecy can be seen in the life of Solomon. David wanted to build a temple for God, but God told him that Solomon would build the Temple, and also that "…I [God] will establish his kingdom." The prophet Nathan foretold the establishment of Solomon's kingdom.

2 Samuel 7:12 and 13

(12) When your days are over and you rest with your fathers, I will raise up your offspring to succeed you, who will come from your own body, and **I will establish his kingdom.**

(13) He is the one who will build a house for my Name, and I will establish the throne of his kingdom forever.[2]

These prophetic words seem very final. However, Solomon got to the point in his life where he did great evil in the eyes of God and broke commandment after commandment. God commanded that the king not amass silver and gold, but Solomon received 666 talents (more than 49,000 pounds) of gold a year (Deut. 17:17; 1 Kings 10:14). God commanded that the king not amass horses or get horses from Egypt, but Solomon had thousands of horses, many of them from Egypt (Deut. 17:16; 1 Kings 10:26-29). God commanded that the king not have many wives, but Solomon had 700 wives and 300 concubines (Deut. 17:17; 1 Kings 11:3). God commanded that no Israelite marry a pagan woman, but Solomon married "Moabites, Ammonites, Edomites, Sidonians, and Hittites" (1 Kings 11:1 and 2). God

> We know that prophecy spoken to people is often conditional.

commanded all Israel to stay away from idolatry (which was the first of the Ten Commandments), but Solomon worshipped Ashtoreth and Molech, among other pagan gods (1 Kings 11:5). Solomon "did evil" in the eyes of God (1 Kings 11:6), and after much sin, a different prophetic word came to him:

1 Kings 11:11

So the LORD said to Solomon, "Since this is your attitude and you

---

2. This prophecy will ultimately be fulfilled in Jesus Christ. The "throne" of Solomon's kingdom will eventually, and then everlastingly, be occupied by Jesus.

have not kept my covenant and my decrees, which I commanded you, **I will most certainly tear the kingdom away from you** and give it to one of your subordinates.

Because Solomon disobeyed and turned from the commands of God, the kingdom, which God prophesied He would "establish," was torn from David's line. Only two tribes, Judah and Benjamin, became the kingdom of Judah. The ten northern tribes became their own kingdom, Israel.

Rehoboam's deliverance from Shishak. Solomon abandoned God and, as a result, the kingdom was torn from him. Sadly, his son Rehoboam did not learn from his father's mistakes and continued in his profligate ways. He and his people further abandoned God, and as a result God's protection was taken away. Shishak, Pharaoh of Egypt, came and attacked Jerusalem. When the prophet Shemaiah foretold that God would abandon the kingdom of Judah to Pharaoh Shishak, everything seemed lost.

2 Chronicles 12:1 and 5
(1) After Rehoboam's position as king was established and he had become strong, he and all Israel with him abandoned the law of the LORD.
(5) Then the prophet Shemaiah came to Rehoboam and to the leaders of Judah who had assembled in Jerusalem for fear of Shishak, and he said to them, "This is what the LORD says, **'You have abandoned me; therefore, I now abandon you to Shishak.'"**

The proclamation that God would abandon Israel to the Egyptians seemed final, but the leaders of Israel understood its conditional nature and did not consider it the "final word." They humbled themselves before God, and as a result, the prophecy concerning Judah was not fulfilled. God sent Shemaiah back with a new prophecy that even foretold "deliverance."

2 Chronicles 12:6 and 7
(6) The leaders of Israel and the king humbled themselves and said, "The LORD is just."

(7) When the LORD saw that they humbled themselves, this word of the LORD came to Shemaiah: "Since they have humbled themselves, **I will not destroy them** but will soon give them deliverance. My wrath will not be poured out on Jerusalem through Shishak."

In this case, the fact that the leaders of Judah understood the conditional nature of prophecy saved their kingdom. Had they believed that the first prophecy from Shemaiah could not be changed, they would not have humbled themselves and repented as they did.

Disaster on Ahab. In 1 Kings 21, the evil King Ahab, husband to the infamous Jezebel, did nothing while an innocent man and his family were murdered by executive order. Elijah the prophet came to Ahab with a word from God.

1 Kings 21:21 and 22
(21) "**I am going to bring disaster on you**. I will consume your descendants and cut off from Ahab every last male in Israel—slave or free.
(22) I will make your house like that of Jeroboam son of Nebat and that of Baasha son of Ahijah, because you have provoked me to anger and have caused Israel to sin."

As evil as he was, Ahab realized he was in serious trouble. Elijah foretold disaster on "you," i.e., Ahab, and also on his "house." The "houses" of Jeroboam and Baasha whom Elijah mentioned, both former kings of Israel, had been totally destroyed. Ahab knew he was doomed if something did not change, and he acted decisively:

1 Kings 21:27-29
(27) When Ahab heard these words, he tore his clothes, put on sackcloth and fasted. He lay in sackcloth and went around meekly.
(28) Then the word of the LORD came to Elijah the Tishbite:
(29) "Have you noticed how Ahab has humbled himself before me? Because he has humbled himself, **I will not bring this disaster in**

his day, but I will bring it on his house in the days of his son."

When Elijah foretold Ahab's disaster, Ahab did not shrug his shoulders and say, "Well, the word of God has come. I'm history." No, he understood that prophecy could be conditional, and thought that if he changed his behavior, the word of God might change. In his case, it did, and God told Elijah that He would not bring disaster on Ahab as He had said, but would delay it until the reign of Ahab's son. We can only speculate what would have happened if Ahab's son had also repented and lived a godly life, but the chances are that the prophecy would have been altered again. As it was, Ahab's son, Ahaziah, died childless after falling out a window, and his brother Joram took over the throne. Joram also did evil in the eyes of God, and Jehu, a commander in the army, killed him and destroyed the house of Ahab, fulfilling the prophecy that destruction would come in the "days of his son."

Hezekiah's sickness. Another example of God changing His revelation when people act decisively is in 2 Kings 20. Hezekiah, king of Judah, was very sick. The prophet Isaiah came to him and said, "…Put your house in order, because you are going to die; you will not recover" (2 Kings 20:1). As final as that prophecy from Isaiah sounded, Hezekiah did not give up. He prayed and wept, and God spoke again to Isaiah.

2 Kings 20:5a
"Go back and tell Hezekiah, the leader of my people, 'This is what the LORD, the God of your father David, says: I have heard your prayer and seen your tears; I will heal you…

Hezekiah was healed, even as the second word from God said. The original prophecy that Hezekiah would die was not fulfilled, and he lived another 15 years.

Nineveh's destruction. Another good example of the conditional nature of prophecy is in the book of Jonah. The prophet Jonah delivered the following message to the citizens of Nineveh: "…Forty more days and Nineveh will be overturned" (Jon. 3:4). Although the people of Nineveh had been wicked and the prophecy was clear, the king of Nineveh knew not to simply give up, sit back, and await destruction. He knew that prophecy could be conditional, and so he commanded everyone in his kingdom to repent, fast, and "call urgently on God" (Jon. 3:8). The king even commanded that the animals in the kingdom be made to fast. He then gave his reason for these commands:

Jonah 3:9
"Who knows? God may yet relent and with compassion turn from his fierce anger so that we will not perish."

Although the king had no guarantee that his kingdom would be saved if the people humbled themselves, he knew that if they did not, the prophecy would certainly come to pass and Nineveh would be destroyed. Some prophecies, even when given by a genuine prophet, are not the final word. In the case of Nineveh, the word of God spoken in prophecy changed.

Jonah 3:10
When God saw what they did and how they turned from their evil ways, he had compassion and did not bring upon them the destruction he had threatened.

The NIV text above is a weak translation. First, the phrase "had compassion" is better translated "repented" as it is in the KJV (the NRSV actually has "changed his mind"). This is very important. We said at the opening of this chapter that, in effect, most prophecies spoken to people had an unspoken "if" clause. It can be clearly seen here. When God saw that the people of Nineveh repented and turned from their evil ways, then He "repented." God changed His word when the circumstances changed.

Also, although the NIV has the word "threatened," there is no evidence in the Hebrew text that all God did was "threaten" the Ninevites. God plainly stated that Nineveh would be overthrown. The Hebrew is clearly translated in many versions, the King James being one of them, and it is worth quoting.

Jonah 3:10 (KJV)
And God saw their works, that they turned from their evil way; and God repented of the evil, that he had said that he would do unto them; and he did *it* not.

It is worth noting, however, that the translators of the NIV have picked up the heart of what God did. Although with words He clearly stated that Nineveh would be overthrown, in His heart He did not want that to happen. His words were a "threat," even though they were not voiced that way, because He intended to change if the Ninevites did. When they repented, He did not bring upon them the destruction that Jonah had so boldly proclaimed. The prophecy of Jonah, that Nineveh would be destroyed in 40 days, was never fulfilled.

Josiah's death. Still another example of the conditional nature of prophecy is the prophecy of Huldah the prophetess concerning Josiah, king of Judah. Josiah had been very aggressive in restoring the worship of the true God in Judah. Under his reign, the Temple was repaired, and in the process, the scrolls containing the Word of God were found. The previous king had been ungodly, and the Law had been grossly neglected. Josiah had the scrolls read to him and was alarmed at his people's disobedience to the Law. He sent a messenger to the prophetess to hear from God what would happen to his kingdom because the Law had been so neglected. Huldah said that the kingdom would suffer disaster, but not at that time. Concerning Josiah himself she said:

2 Kings 22:20 (NASB)
"Therefore, behold, I will gather you to your fathers, and **you will be gathered to your grave in peace,** neither shall your eyes see all the evil which I will bring on this place.'" "So they brought back word to the king.

Josiah had received a blessing from God. He would be "gathered to his fathers" a phrase almost always used of a peaceful death. Furthermore, it would be "in peace." However, Josiah disobeyed God and entered into a war with Pharaoh Neco, king of Egypt. The Pharaoh was traveling north through Judah to fight the Babylonians and did not want to go to war with Josiah. In fact, when Josiah came out with his armies, Pharaoh tried to get Josiah to leave him alone.

2 Chronicles 35:20-22

(20) After all this, when Josiah had set the temple in order, Neco king of Egypt went up to fight at Carchemish on the Euphrates, and Josiah marched out to meet him in battle.

(21) But Neco sent messengers to him, saying, "What quarrel is there between you and me, O king of Judah? It is not you I am attacking at this time, but the house with which I am at war. God has told me to hurry; so stop opposing God, who is with me, or he will destroy you."

(22) Josiah, however, would not turn away from him, but disguised himself to engage him in battle. He would not listen to what Neco had said at God's command but went to fight him on the plain of Megiddo.

Josiah was so intent on fighting Pharaoh that he paid no attention to God. He even disguised himself so he could fight without being recognized as the king of Judah, so that there would be no chance Pharaoh Neco could protect him by telling his soldiers not to fight the king. His bold disobedience put him in danger, and he was shot by an arrow and died slowly, miles from the battleground.

2 Chronicles 35:23 and 24a

(23) Archers shot King Josiah, and he told his officers, "Take me away; I am badly wounded."

(24a) So they took him out of his chariot, put him in the other chariot he had and brought him to Jerusalem, where he died...

Josiah disobeyed God and entered into battle, and died as a result. What about the prophecy that he would be gathered to his fathers and die in "peace"? Like other prophecies, it was conditional upon obedience to God. Had Josiah not disobeyed and entered into a war he had no business fighting, he would have died in peace just as Huldah foretold.

But because Josiah disobeyed God, the words of Huldah, who was a genuine prophetess of God, did not come to pass.

There is an important lesson that we should learn from Josiah. The prophecy that he would die "in peace" did not make him invincible, as if he could then do anything no matter how foolhardy, and live through it. The prophecy would have been fulfilled if he had lived wisely, in obedience to God. Similarly, if a Christian receives a prophecy of blessing, he usually must be wise and godly to see it fulfilled in his life.

Zedekiah's death. Another clear example of the conditional nature of prophecy is in the book of Jeremiah. Zedekiah was the last king of Judah before the Babylonian captivity. He had the chance to save his kingdom by surrendering to Nebuchadnezzar, the king of Babylon, but he did not surrender. When Nebuchadnezzar's army surrounded Jerusalem, Zedekiah made a proclamation that everyone in the city was to free his slaves (Jer. 34:8-10). The slaves were supposed to be released every seven years, as the Law of Moses declared (Exod. 21:2), but the people of Judah had been disobedient in that area. It blessed God when Zedekiah released the slaves, and He sent Jeremiah to tell the king that even though Jerusalem would be burned and he would be captured, he would die in peace.

Jeremiah 34:4 and 5
(4) "'Yet hear the promise of the LORD, O Zedekiah king of Judah. This is what the LORD says concerning you: You will not die by the sword;
(5) **you will die peacefully**. As people made a funeral fire in honor of your fathers, the former kings who preceded you, so they will make a fire in your honor and lament, "Alas, O master!" I myself make this promise, declares the LORD.'"

The word from God was that Zedekiah would "die peacefully" and people would make a funeral fire for him. However, before long the people of Judah "...changed their minds and took back the slaves they had freed and enslaved them again" (Jer. 34:11). They also sinned in many other ways. Because of the wicked sin of Zedekiah and the people of Judah,

Jeremiah was sent back to the king with a different message:

Jeremiah 34:17, 19-21

(17) Therefore, this is what the LORD says: 'You have not obeyed me; you have not proclaimed freedom for your fellow countrymen. So I now proclaim 'freedom' for you, declares the LORD —'freedom' to fall by the sword, plague and famine. I will make you abhorrent to all the kingdoms of the earth.

(19) The leaders of Judah and Jerusalem, the court officials, the priests and all the people of the land who walked between the pieces of the calf,

(20) I will hand over to their enemies who seek their lives. Their dead bodies will become food for the birds of the air and the beasts of the earth.

(21) I will hand Zedekiah king of Judah and his officials over to their enemies who seek their lives, to the army of the king of Babylon, which has withdrawn from you."

God had said that Zedekiah would die "peacefully" and that people would make a fire in honor of him and lament for him. But after his grievous sin, God spoke a different word—that he would be handed over to his enemies. Had Zedekiah repented in sackcloth and ashes like Ahab and others had done, perhaps the word from God would have changed yet again. However, he continued in his wicked ways and the second word from God was fulfilled:

Jeremiah 52:10 and 11

(10) There at Riblah the king of Babylon slaughtered the sons of Zedekiah before his eyes; he also killed all the officials of Judah.

(11) Then he put out Zedekiah's eyes, bound him with bronze shackles and took him to Babylon, where he put him in prison till the day of his death.

Zedekiah could have died in peace as the first prophecy said, but he, like many others, abandoned his godly acts and turned to wickedness, so instead of being fulfilled, the first prophecy was set aside by a later prophecy. The last thing Zedekiah saw before the Babylonians blinded him was his sons being put to death, and then, blinded, he was taken in chains to Babylon where he died in prison. Dying in a prison blind and in chains is certainly not dying "peacefully," as Jeremiah's original prophecy stated. This record in Jeremiah is more evidence that much prophecy is conditional in nature and based on the attitude and actions of the believer.

Prophecies That Did Not Change

What follows are two examples of people praying to God so that the prophecies they received would be altered, but they were not, and came to pass as spoken. Just because prophecy is often conditional does not mean it always is. Nevertheless, the preponderance of examples in the Word of God teach us that if we receive a prophecy we do not want to come to pass, we should do all that we can to alter the prophecy.

The death of David's child. David committed adultery with a woman named Bathsheba, who became pregnant and gave birth to a son. While the son was very young, but not a newborn, God gave the following prophecy to David:

2 Samuel 12:14b
...the son born to you will die.

After the prophecy was given, the child became sick. David pleaded with God to spare the child. He fasted and "...spent the nights lying on the ground." However, the child died anyway, at which point David washed, went to worship, and then ate. This confused the servants, who wondered why David did not fast and weep after the death of the child, and they asked him about it.

2 Samuel 12:22
He answered, "While the child was still alive, I fasted and wept.

I thought, 'Who knows? The LORD may be gracious to me and let the child live.'

David understood that even though God had given a prophecy that the child would die, there was a chance he might live. He prayed and fasted, asking God to alter the consequences of his sin. The fact that David fasted, wept, and spent the nights lying on the ground, is an indication that he knew that the prophecy of the death of the child was not absolutely set in stone, but might change. In this case, however, the prophecy came to pass as spoken.

Jesus in Gethsemane. One of the most startling examples of the conditional nature of prophecy involves Jesus Christ. On the night of his arrest, he went to the Garden of Gethsemane and prayed three times that he would not have to die. The prayer recorded in Mark is very telling:

Mark 14:36
"*Abba*, Father," he said, "everything is possible for you. Take this cup from me. Yet not what I will, but what you will."

Jesus began his prayer by saying that everything is possible for God. What he had in mind was obvious from his next statement—that perhaps God could change what had been foretold about the death of the Messiah. Jesus boldly asked God, "…Take this cup from me…." What was Jesus asking for? He was asking God to change things so that he would not have to be tortured and die. This shows that Jesus clearly understood the conditional nature of prophecy. He knew that even though his death had been foretold, that did not necessarily mean it was absolutely set in stone, and he prayed to see if there was any way that redemption could be accomplished without his death. The fact that he prayed three times showed how badly he wanted to avoid being tortured and crucified. However, in this case, there was apparently no way God could bring about the redemption of mankind except by the death of Jesus, and Jesus humbly accepted that fact and died for our sins. What a Savior!

This chapter has shown that many prophecies are conditional in nature. Just because someone receives a prophecy does not mean that things cannot change in the future. If a Christian receives a prophecy that states he will have financial deliverance and blessing in his life, he should not think that he can then behave any way he wants to and still be financially secure. Or if a Christian gets a prophecy stating that he is called of God to be the leader of some great endeavor or ministry, he better not think that his position is secure and that God will continue to promote and support him even if he turns from Him. In most cases, the fulfillment of any prophecy that a Christian receives is conditional on continued obedience to God. In the same vein, a Christian should not think that because of past evil behavior he can never receive God's blessing on his life. It would be difficult for a Christian to be as wicked as King Ahab, but God changed the prophecy even for him when he repented.

It is important to note that God does not desire to be seen as a God whose words have no impact because they change all the time. What God says will indeed come to pass unless there are powerful circumstances for them to change. In that light, although there are many examples showing that prophecy can be conditional, there are many more prophecies in the Word of God that were fulfilled as spoken.

CHAPTER THREE
Who Actually Does the Work?

Our Part in Fulfilling Prophecy

Something that has been a source of confusion to Bible students, people who receive revelation, and people who receive prophetic words, is that often when God says "He" will do something, "He" does not. It is vital for anyone who deals with revelation and prophecy, whether it is in the Bible or received personally, to know the following: **when God says He will do something, it almost always means that He will help someone do it.** A very clear example is the way God dealt with the Amalekites. He was very angry with them because when Israel came out of Egypt, they went to the back of the Israelite column and attacked the weak and straggling people. Because of that cowardly and horrible act, God said he would destroy the Amalekites completely.

Exodus 17:14
Then the LORD said to Moses, "Write this on a scroll as something to be remembered and make sure that Joshua hears it, because **I will** completely blot out the memory of Amalek from under heaven."

This verse seems very clear and self-explanatory: God is going to deal with the Amalekites Himself. However, 40 years later God had done nothing and Joshua was about to go into the Promised Land where the Amalekites lived. In the last two months of the wilderness wandering, God spoke again about the Amalekites, and it seems as if He changed His mind. He said to Moses:

Deuteronomy 25:17-19
(17) Remember what the Amalekites did to you along the way when you came out of Egypt.
(18) When you were weary and worn out, they met you on your journey and cut off all who were lagging behind; they had no fear of God.

(19) When the LORD your God gives you rest from all the enemies around you in the land he is giving you to possess as an inheritance, you shall blot out the memory of Amalek from under heaven. Do not forget!

Wait a minute! Why did God tell Israel, "…**you shall** blot out the memory of Amalek…" when earlier He had said that **He would** do it. Did He change His mind? A study of Scripture reveals that He did not change His mind. It is a fact of prophetic vocabulary, both in the Bible and today, that when God says He will do something, it usually means that He will give us divine support as we do it. There are many examples of that in the Bible, and this chapter does not contain an exhaustive list of them. Nevertheless, the examples in it are clear, and make the point that in prophetic language, God saying He will do something does not mean He will do it without a concerted effort on our part.

In the book of Exodus, God said that He would wipe out the Canaanites in the Promised Land:

Exodus 23:23
My angel will go ahead of you and bring you into the land of the Amorites, Hittites, Perizzites, Canaanites, Hivites and Jebusites, and **I will** wipe them out.

Once again, this seems to be clear and self-explanatory language. The real meaning, however, is revealed a few verses later.

Exodus 23:31
"I will establish your borders from the Red Sea to the Sea of the Philistines, and from the desert to the River. I will hand over to you the people who live in the land and **you will** drive them out before you.

We learn from verse 31 that God expected the Israelites to drive out the Canaanites. Why then did He say that He would do it? Because He was both revealing His will for Israel and adding that He would support their efforts. But the Israelites did not obey God and drive out the Canaanites. In fact, the book of Judges reveals that they allowed Canaanites to live all over the Promised Land. So what happened to God's statement that "…I will wipe them out"? It did not get accomplished. God's prophetic statements about what **He will do** are actually about what **He will help people do**, and if they do not do it, then what God wanted to accomplish just does not get done.

Another interesting example occurs in the book of Leviticus.

Leviticus 20:1-3
(1) The LORD said to Moses,
(2) "Say to the Israelites: 'Any Israelite or any alien living in Israel who gives any of his children to Molech must be put to death. **The people of the community are to stone him.**
(3) I will set my face against that man and **I will cut him off from his people**; for by giving his children to Molech, he has defiled my sanctuary and profaned my holy name.

Note that in verse 2 the command of God is that the people of Israel are to stone to death any person who sacrifices his children to Molech. The people do the actual execution. Nevertheless, in verse 3 God says, "…I will cut him [the guilty one] off…." So we learn that being executed by the men of Israel was equivalent to being "cut off," by God. When God says He did it, He meant that He did it through His agents, in this case His people.

Another example comes from the Israelites' experience with manna, a supernatural food that God gave them while they were in the desert. Manna appeared on the ground like frost all around the camp of Israel, and when the sun came up and the day got hot, which is quite early in the morning in the desert, it melted (Exod. 16:14 and 21). It took diligence and work to gather it (imagine trying to gather enough frost to feed your family). The people had to be careful gathering it or they would get sand mixed in with it—not a very pleasant dining experience. Furthermore, if anyone slept in, he went hungry that day. Little wonder the Israelites occasionally attributed their full stomachs to their own ability.

Deuteronomy 8:16-18

(16) He gave you manna to eat in the desert, something your fathers had never known, to humble and to test you so that in the end it might go well with you.

(17) You may say to yourself, "My power and the strength of my hands have produced this wealth for me."

(18) But remember the LORD your God, for it is he who gives you the ability to produce wealth, and so confirms his covenant, which he swore to your forefathers, as it is today.

The Israelites worked hard in order to eat, even though the manna came from heaven. Nevertheless, Scripture said that God was "feeding you with manna" (Deut. 8:3) as if it really involved no effort at all. The truth is revealed in verse 18 above, that God gives us "...the ability to produce wealth...." Because He gives us the ability to get wealth and the availability of it, when we work hard and prosper, it is still legitimate for God to say that He did it.

We live in a time when the Christian Church is increasingly recognizing prophets and prophetic ministry. A person can go to any number of churches today and get a prophecy, and God uses prophetic vocabulary today in the same way He has used it in ages past. A person might well receive a prophecy that he will get out of debt, or his home church will increase in number, or he will be brought before great men, or he will receive greater understanding of the Bible. In each of these cases it should be clear that what was prophesied will not happen without the person who received the prophecy working to make it come to pass. God has stated His intention to make the work successful, and assure the person that the task ahead of him is not of his own invention. Now God and the person both work to make what was spoken come to pass.

The Need For Wisdom

We have just seen that when God says He will do something, He usually means that He will give us strength and support as we do the work. This explains why verses such as Philippians 4:19 (which says that

"...God will meet all your needs...") go unfulfilled in the lives of some Christians. Many a pastor has sat with a disappointed person whose life is a mess and heard him say something like this: "I just don't understand it. God says He will meet all my needs. Why isn't He coming through for me?" Many pastors do not know what to say at that point because they, too, are confused by the promise and the apparent lack of its fulfillment.[1] Christians need to know that when God says He will meet all our needs, He is using the same type of vocabulary that He uses all through Scripture: He will work to fulfill His Word as we work with Him using the wisdom and abilities He gave us. We have to be wise and work.

The Bible has hundreds of verses extolling the value of wisdom. Proverbs alone mentions "wisdom" more than 50 times, and "wise" 60 times. The successful Christian learns how wisdom, revelation, and prophetic input work together. The Bible tells us that "Wisdom is supreme; therefore get wisdom. Though it cost all you have, get understanding" (Prov. 4:7). Think about what it took for Joshua and the Israelites to fulfill God's promise that He would wipe out the Canaanites. The Israelite army did not sit and have a picnic while God worked. They fought hard, and it took faith, prayer, planning, wisdom, hard work, risk, time, and even some Israelite blood spilled. Even with all that, Israel did not conquer the whole land because they did not have the heart and faith to finish the job.

The promise that God will meet all our needs is no different. It takes

---

1. Unfortunately, at this point many pastors assume that God is meeting the person's needs and thus counsel him to try to see things "from God's point of view." This kind of poor pastoral counseling has left many people hurt and confused, thinking that God's definition of "needs" must be different from the ordinary definition. That is not the case. The Bible is not written in code, and God's use of words such as "needs," "love," "good," etc., is no different from our ordinary use. The problem is that we do not know how God works with us to bring about His purposes, and sometimes we erroneously believe that God's purposes for us will happen no matter what we do. For more on the fact that God is not in control of everything that happens on earth and that He needs us to work with Him, see our book, *Don't Blame God! A Biblical Answer to the Problem of Evil, Sin and Suffering* by Mark Graeser, John Lynn, John Schoenheit, (Christian Educational Services, Indianapolis, IN, 2005). To read key sections/chapters of this book online, go to www.TruthOrTradition.com TOPIC: Don't Blame God.

hard work and wisdom on our part. If a person wants all his needs met, he must be prepared to be as single-minded and wise as Joshua was about conquering Canaan. Similarly, if a person gets a prophetic word that God will clear a path for him, he must put his clearing clothes on and get his clearing tools out. God wants the job done, and will empower the individual, who will be doing the sweating. If God says He will bring a person before great men, that person should start thinking of ways to meet some of them. God will give support, but the individual must do his part.

There are some occasions in the Word when God says He will do something, and then does it Himself without human help. However, these are rare compared to the times when He works through people. If a person receives a prophetic word and cannot decide whether God wants him to stand aside and let Him work or to do the work with divine support, he should pray and get counsel. That is a good reason to have prophecies recorded. Others can listen and give wise counsel and spiritual insight.

The need to use wisdom in order to have God's promises fulfilled is very important. From Genesis until today there have been countless times God has told an individual what He wants to do, but it is up to that person to have faith and use wisdom to carry it out. When God lets us know what He wants, He often reveals the "Big Picture," i.e., the overall picture, and we then must fill in the details using wisdom. For example, in Genesis 12 God told Abraham to leave his home and go to a land He would reveal to him. Do you think Abraham took time to plan the trip? Certainly. God did not have to tell him to take money and provisions with him, and travel at a favorable time of year. That is simply the wise thing to do.

> The need to use wisdom in order to have God's promises fulfilled is very important.

Joshua had revelation to conquer the Promised Land. Did he have to use wisdom and planning? You bet he did. God told Gideon to tear down the altar of Baal that his father owned, but it was Gideon's decision to destroy it at night when the men who worshipped there could not see it being done (Judg. 6:25-27). God told King Saul to attack the Amalekites and destroy them (1 Sam. 15:3), but Saul had to come up with the battle plan. God gave David the revelation as to when to attack the Philistines (2 Sam. 5:19), but David, as any military leader would, had a wisely conceived battle plan—after all, he had led armies for many years.

The point of the above examples, which could be multiplied many times over from both Scripture and personal experience, is that when someone gets a revelation to do something, that person still needs to use wisdom to accomplish what God told him to do. If you do not, you will more than likely end up like Israel conquering Canaan—even though the revelation was clear, the job will not get done. In order to be truly successful in life, we need to hear from God what He wants done, and then we need to put together a wise plan of action to bring God's will to pass on earth.

CHAPTER FOUR
The Christian and the Manifestation of Prophecy

Every Christian Can Prophesy

Every Christian has the God-given ability to prophesy. As we saw in Chapter One, prophecy is a manifestation of the gift of holy spirit, which each Christian receives the moment he is born again. The presence of holy spirit in a believer gives him the ability to prophesy. 1 Corinthians 14:1, quoted at the opening of this book, says that every believer should follow after spiritual things, especially prophecy. A few verses later, verse 5a says that God wants every believer to prophesy.

> **1 Corinthians 14:5a**
> I would like every one of you to speak in tongues, but I would rather have you prophesy...

This verse shows that God wants each Christian to both speak in tongues and prophesy. Other verses show this truth also.

> **1 Corinthians 14:24**
> But if an unbeliever or someone who does not understand comes in while **everybody** is prophesying, he will be convinced by all that he is a sinner and will be judged by all,

"**Everybody**" means **everybody**. The whole Church can prophesy if they want to and are taught how to bring it forth. Another verse that says all Christians can prophesy is: "Therefore, my brothers, be eager to prophesy…" (1 Cor. 14:39a). The fact that this was written to the "brothers" and not just to a select few in the Church is more clear evidence that all Christians can prophesy.

Every Christian can prophesy today because every Christian has the gift of holy spirit. This was not the case in the Old Testament and the Four Gospels because before the Day of Pentecost (Acts 2), God gave holy spirit to only a small percent of the people, and only those people could prophesy. The book of Numbers shows the correlation between having holy spirit and being able to prophesy. The record we will now examine occurred during Israel's wilderness wanderings. Moses had holy spirit, so he could hear from God, but apparently no one else did. Moses was carrying the spiritual burden of Israel all by himself, and he pleaded for God to help.

Numbers 11:14 and 15

(14) [Moses said], "I cannot carry all these people by myself; the burden is too heavy for me.

(15) If this is how you are going to treat me, put me to death right now—if I have found favor in your eyes—and do not let me face my own ruin."

God answered Moses' plea by putting holy spirit on 70 other men, not a large number considering the millions of Israelites. The presence of the spirit of God empowered those who had it, and immediately they manifested some of that power by prophesying.

Numbers 11:16 and 17, 24 and 25a

(16) The LORD said to Moses: "Bring me seventy of Israel's elders who are known to you as leaders and officials among the people. Have them come to the Tent of Meeting, that they may stand there with you.

(17) I will come down and speak with you there, and I will take of the Spirit [spirit] that is on you and put the Spirit [spirit] on them. They will help you carry the burden of the people so that you will not have to carry it alone.

(24) So Moses went out and told the people what the LORD had said. He brought together seventy of their elders and had them stand around the Tent.

(25a) Then the LORD came down in the cloud and spoke with him, and he [He] took of the Spirit [spirit] that was on him [Moses] and put the Spirit [spirit] on the seventy elders. **When the Spirit [spirit] rested on them, they prophesied**...

For reasons we are not told in the biblical record, two of the seventy men remained in the camp of Israel and did not go out to the Tent of Meeting. Even upon them, however, God's holy spirit rested, and they prophesied. This alarmed Moses' aide, Joshua, who told Moses to stop them.

Numbers 11:26-28
(26) However, two men, whose names were Eldad and Medad, had remained in the camp. They were listed among the elders, but did not go out to the Tent. Yet **the Spirit [spirit] also rested on them, and they prophesied** in the camp.
(27) A young man ran and told Moses, "Eldad and Medad are prophesying in the camp."
(28) Joshua son of Nun, who had been Moses' aide since youth, spoke up and said, "Moses, my lord, stop them!"

Moses' answered Joshua with a wish—one that now, in the Grace Administration, has come to pass.[1]

Numbers 11:29
But Moses replied, "Are you jealous for my sake? I wish that all the LORD's people were prophets and that the LORD would put his Spirit [spirit] on them!"

Moses wished that all of God's people would have holy spirit on them so that every person could hear directly from God and prophesy. Moses' desire has now come to pass. Every Christian is filled with the gift of holy spirit and can prophesy. It is clear from this record in the book of Numbers that when the spirit from God was put on someone, that person

---

1. Understanding the Administrations in the Bible is vital for understanding the Bible. The Administration of Grace started on the Day of Pentecost (Acts 2) and will end with the Rapture, when both dead and still-living Christians meet the Lord in the air (1 Thess. 4:13-18). For more on Administrations in the Bible, see our booklet, *Defending Dispensationalism* (Christian Educational Services, Indianapolis, IN, 2001) and our book, *The Christian's Hope: The Anchor of the Soul* by John Schoenheit (Christian Educational Services, Indianapolis, IN, 2004), pp. 201-220. You can read *Defending Dispensationalism* online at www.TruthOrTradition.com TOPIC: Administrations.

could prophesy. This is confirmed in many places in the Old Testament.

Acts 19 contains an example from the Administration of Grace showing that when people receive holy spirit, they can prophesy.

Acts 19:6
When Paul placed his hands on them, the Holy Spirit [No article "the," should read "holy spirit."] came on them, and they spoke in tongues and prophesied.

Although not every person who gets born again speaks in tongues and prophesies right away, in this case apparently they did. However, there are several things that could have occurred. The word "and" indicates continuance, but not necessarily immediate continuance. It is possible that between the first and last clauses in the verse, there was some time for Paul to instruct the disciples in the operation of the manifestations. It is also possible that God was gracious and gave supernatural understanding or inspiration to them. A third possibility is that they knew from their culture how manifestations of holy spirit worked, especially prophecy, and when they knew that they had the ability from the Lord to manifest, they just stepped out in faith and began. Some Christians who speak in tongues around their home and take their small children to meetings where people regularly speak in tongues and prophesy report that their children start manifesting the holy spirit naturally, with no formal instruction.

Long before the Christian era, God promised that there was a day coming when "all flesh," every person, would have holy spirit and be able to prophesy.

Joel 2:28 and 29
(28) And afterward, I will pour out my Spirit [spirit] on all people. Your sons and daughters will prophesy, your old men will dream dreams,[2] your young men will see visions.
(29) Even on my servants, both men and women, I will pour out my Spirit [spirit] in those days.

---

2. For more on "dreams," see Appendix C, *Dreams.*

The people of the Old Testament knew the power a person had when holy spirit was upon him. They had seen or heard of many people who had holy spirit and who walked in power, such as Moses, Joshua, Ehud, Deborah, Gideon, Samson, Samuel, David, Elijah, and Elisha. A person with the spirit of God was someone to be reckoned with. He could hear from God and manifest the power of God. Prophecy was an important part of what someone with holy spirit could do, and the Old Testament prophets had walked in holy spirit power for centuries.

> Long before the Christian era, God promised that there was a day coming when "all flesh," every person, would have holy spirit and be able to prophesy.

God promised that there was a day coming when every believer would have the gift of holy spirit (Joel 2:28).[3] This prophecy in Joel refers specifically to the believers in the Millennial Kingdom.[4] On the Day of Pentecost, however, God gave the gift of holy spirit to the Christian Church, and with that gift came the ability to prophesy. In fact, on Pentecost, Peter added to the words of Joel. Whereas Joel said, "Even on my servants, both men and women, I will pour out my Spirit [spirit] in those days," Peter expanded it to "Even on my servants, both men and women, I will pour out my Spirit [spirit] in those days, **and they will prophesy**" (Acts 2:18).

It is clear from Joel and other scriptures that when a person has the spirit of God, he can prophesy just as the prophets in the Old Testament

---

3. Although the verse in Joel says, "all flesh," that is the limited use of "all" and means "all who are believers." This conclusion can be supported in several different ways, but the clearest is Jesus' words in John 7:39 that holy spirit would be given to those who believe. For more on the limited sense of "all," see our book, Appendix A, (Col. 1:15-20, note 5), *One God & One Lord: Reconsidering the Cornerstone of the Christian Faith* by Mark Graeser, John Lynn, & John Schoenheit (Christian Educational Services, Indianapolis, IN, 2003), pp. 510 and 511. This appendix is posted on www.BiblicalUnitarian.com in its entirety.

4. For more about the Millennial Kingdom and what it will be like, see our book, *op. cit., The Christian's Hope* or visit www.TruthOrTradition.com TOPIC: Christian's Hope.

did. There is no indication that the spirit of God in each Christian has less power than the holy spirit that was upon the Old Testament prophets. In fact, the gift of holy spirit born inside Christians is the fullness of the spirit, not just a portion of it as it was with the Old Testament believers who had holy spirit upon them. This is an important point because there are Christians who admit that prophecy is a manifestation of holy spirit available to every Christian, but who believe that the manifestation of prophecy is only for groups (corporate prophecy), not individuals, and also that it is not for guidance or direction, but only general statements of strengthening, encouragement, and comfort. That is not the case.

Prophecy is prophecy, and when a Christian receives holy spirit he is empowered to prophesy just as the Old Testament prophets were. Whether or not he does so is based on his personal faith and his individual God-given ministry. 1 Corinthians 14:24 and 25 refers to the fact that the whole Church can prophesy and uncover the secrets of people's hearts. It makes sense that the whole church can prophesy because each person making up the congregation has holy spirit. Thus we can safely conclude that God has given every Christian the ability to prophesy. However, the message that they bring forth is the message that God gives them, and Scripture tells us that in the manifestation of prophecy the message will fall in the general category of "edification, exhortation, and comfort" (1 Cor. 14:3-KJV).

On the Day of Pentecost, and for the next several decades, people manifested the spirit because they were claiming the promise of the spirit as it was given in Joel, Isaiah, and other places in the Old Testament. However, as the Church Epistles were written, starting about 50 A.D., Christians learned that we are part of a new administration called the Administration of the Sacred Secret.[5] We now know we are children of

---

5. For more information on the Sacred Secret see, "Appendix A," "The Administration of the Sacred Secret" in our book, *op cit. The Gift of Holy Spirit* by Mark Graeser, John Lynn, and John Schoenheit, our July 2005 Tape of the Month: An Overview Of The Sacred Secret, and *The Sower* magazine Jul/Aug 2005 available online at www.TruthOrTradition.com TOPIC: News. Also see the following TOPICS: Administrations 1 and 2.

God by birth, and some of the blessings we enjoy go beyond the things foretold in the Old Testament. What we have today includes God's gift of holy spirit and the God-given ability that holy spirit brings, including two manifestations unforeseen in the Old Testament: speaking in tongues and the interpretation of tongues.

Not only is each Christian empowered by holy spirit in ways that were unknown and unforeseen in the Old Testament, but the relationship between Christians and God has changed from the relationship people had with Him in Old Testament times. Before Pentecost, God placed holy spirit upon people to empower them for certain tasks. For example, He placed holy spirit on prophets so they could bring messages to the people, and on some kings, such as David, so they would be spiritually equipped to rule. The gift of holy spirit empowers Christians in many ways, and, as we have seen, one of those ways is the ability to prophesy.

Many people who do not believe they can prophesy come to that belief because they are taught that they do not have the "gift" of prophecy. Prophecy is not a "gift," and is never called a gift in correct translations of the Bible. However, there are versions of the Bible that call prophecy a "gift," and this has misled thousands of Christians. Let us compare 1 Corinthians 14:1 in two popular versions, the *King James Version* and the *New International Version*:

1 Corinthians 14:1 (KJV)
Follow after charity, and desire spiritual *gifts*, but rather that ye may prophesy.

1 Corinthians 14:1
Follow the way of love and eagerly desire spiritual gifts, especially the gift of prophecy.

Note that in the NIV, the word "gift" appears twice, and prophecy is called a "gift." However, in the KJV, which in this case follows the Greek text much more closely, prophecy is not called a "gift." Furthermore, in the phrase, "desire spiritual *gifts*," the word "*gifts*" is in *italics*. The words in *italics* in the KJV are not in the original Greek text. The translators of the KJV wanted readers to know that they added those words (supposedly for clarity) to the Bible so they put the added words in *italics*. In other words, a correct reading of the KJV shows that the word "*gifts*" does not appear in the Greek text at all.[6] If a Bible student will search the Scripture for "*gift*" of prophecy, he will find that it **never** appears in the Hebrew, Aramaic, or Greek text. In every case it was added by translators who thought that prophecy was a gift and who then added their theology to the text. A more accurate rendering of 1 Corinthians 14:1 would have "spiritual *things*" rather than "spiritual *gifts*."

Once a Christian understands that prophecy is not a gift but a manifestation of the gift of holy spirit, and also understands that every Christian gets filled with holy spirit at the time he is saved, then it becomes clear why it is that every Christian can prophesy.

Every Christian Should Want to Prophesy

It is one thing for a Christian to know he can prophesy, but it is another thing to desire to do it. God tells us to desire to prophesy.

1 Corinthians 14:1 (NASB)
Pursue love, yet **desire earnestly** spiritual *gifts,* but especially that you may prophesy.

1 Corinthians 14:39 (NASB)
Therefore, my brethren, **desire earnestly to prophesy**, and do not forbid to speak in tongues.

God wants us to earnestly desire to prophesy. There are really two categories of Christians to address at this point: the Christian who has

---

6. The Bible study tools available today make this very easy to check. Bible software programs make checking the Greek text an easy task, and Greek Interlinear texts, such as George R. Berry's *The Interlinear Literal Translation of the Greek New Testament* (Zondervan Publishing House, Grand Rapids, MI, 1971), or Brown, Comfort, and Douglas, *The New Greek English Interlinear New Testament* (Tyndale House Publishers, Inc., Wheaton, IL, 1990) are also easy to use.

never prophesied at all, and the Christian who has prophesied, but rarely does so in meetings.

A Christian who has never prophesied, and who does not particularly want to, needs to take seriously that God clearly tells us to desire to prophesy. God knows that many people are content not to prophesy, which is why He tells us in His Word to desire it. Christians can build the desire to prophesy as they step out and obey God. If a person has never given a prophecy and is unsure about how to get started, we at Spirit & Truth Fellowship International, like some other ministries, instruct people on the manifestation of prophecy.

God always blesses people when they obey, and as we make a practice of doing what He says, the desire will build in our lives. Most Christians know that they should live by what the Bible says whether they feel like it or not. Similarly, most Christians are aware that God will bless them when they obey. The Bible tells us to desire to prophesy, and now it is our turn to step out and obey by prophesying, and build that desire in us.

As well as people who have never prophesied and have no desire to do so, there are also Christians who have prophesied (and thus know they can) but rarely do so because they "do not feel like it," "do not feel led to," or something similar. Often these people are hindered by a fear of failure, or of looking bad, or they have never conquered their hesitation about speaking in public. It is beyond the scope of this work to deal with overcoming fear of failure, fear of speaking in public, or fear of being criticized. If a person is in that category, he should want to obey God so badly that he would seek out pastoral counseling and get help overcoming his fear and hesitation.

There are, however, many people who come to a meeting and then do not prophesy because they do not particularly feel like it at the time. That is one reason why there is sometimes little or no prophecy in church meetings. But why wait to "feel like doing" what God commands? God tells us to pray and, thankfully, most Christians do not wait until He produces a desire in them before they pray. Most Christians know there are occasions when prayer is appropriate, so they pray. Similarly, if the average Christian waited until he had a burning desire to give money to the church before he wrote a check, churches would be a lot poorer. And so it goes with many things of God. The wise Christian reads the Bible, discovers the will of God, and begins to obey whether or not he feels like it.

There is a time to be sensitive to the leading of the Lord when it comes to prophecy. As a Christian overcomes his hesitation about operating the manifestation of prophecy and gets to the point that he earnestly desires to prophesy, then he is more likely to be sensitive to the leading of the Lord about whether or not to prophesy in a particular meeting. If a large number of Christians are gathered to worship, it is not appropriate for everyone to prophesy. When there is a group of people who earnestly desire to prophesy, that is when the *leading* of the Lord becomes very important. In those situations, the Lord is more able to lead the person whom he wants to prophesy to step out and do so. However, if there is a room

> Christians can build the desire to prophesy as they step out and obey God.

full of hesitant people, and no one is stepping forth to prophesy, it is not wrong to prophesy just because the Word of God says you should. It would be similar to what you would do if there were a time for open prayer in the church, but no one would pray. In that situation you would step out boldly and pray because the Bible says to pray, and you would not doubt that it was the will of God. Similarly, the written Word says that Christians are to earnestly desire to prophesy and believers are to seek the building up of the Church (1 Cor. 14:12). It is not wrong to step forth and prophesy in obedience to the written Word, without feeling a leading from the Lord.

Prophecy Builds People's Faith in God

One of the reasons why Christians should be eager to prophesy is because it demonstrates the power of God so that our faith will rest, not only on the written Word, but also on the power of God. Prophecy is one of God's powerful proofs that He exists and that He cares for us.

The Word of God alone is enough for people to have faith in God, but He understands our humanity and wants to give us confirmation. He is a living God and a loving God, and He wants us to have faith that He can work powerfully in our lives. Prophecy can play a large part in helping us realize that. Notice that demonstrating God's power was an important part of Paul's ministry, and it built people's faith.

1 Corinthians 2:4 and 5
(4) My message and my preaching were not with wise and persuasive words, but with a demonstration of the Spirit's power,
(5) so that your faith might not rest on men's wisdom, but on God's power.

1 Thessalonians 1:5
because our gospel came to you not simply with words, but also with power, with the Holy Spirit and with deep conviction. You know how we lived among you for your sake.

1 Corinthians 14:25 tells us that prophecy can so demonstrate the power of God that the one who receives it "…will fall down and worship God, exclaiming, 'God is really among you!'" The faith-building power that prophecy can have is quite amazing.

One of the reasons the Apostle Paul was so effective was that his was much more than a "preaching ministry." Operating the power of God, and teaching others to do so, was also part of his ministry. When the power of God is demonstrated, it not only builds faith, it builds hope:

Romans 15:13
May the God of hope fill you with all joy and peace as you trust in him, so that you may overflow with hope by the power of the Holy Spirit.

A major reason why every Christian should desire to prophesy is because of the powerfully positive effect it can have on others. Of course, it also has a powerful effect on the one prophesying. When a Christian steps out in faith to prophesy, and realizes that he is getting information from Heaven, it can build his faith and give him confidence that he can play an important part in the Lord's plan on earth.

Prophecy Should be Happening in Our Churches

In the Old Testament, when few believers had holy spirit upon them, prophecy[7] was not a regular part of the people's gathering at the Tent of Meeting (Tabernacle) or the Temple. However, the Church Epistles, which are the Lord's direction for his Church, tell us that speaking in tongues with interpretation and prophecy should be occurring regularly in our meetings.[8] This is clear in 1 Corinthians 14. Many Christians go to prophecy conferences or special events where there is prophecy and prophetic ministering, and that is good, but the Lord never meant for prophecy to be only for "big" or "special" conferences. It is also meant to be a part of the home church or fellowship. However, since prophecy and prophetic ministering does not always happen in home churches, there is a blessing in making them available at larger gatherings.

Some Christians Have the Gift Ministry of a Prophet

A major way God communicates with people is through individuals who are specifically called as prophets. They were necessary in the Old Testament and in the early Church, and they are still necessary and present today. God called out the prophets in the Old Testament, but ever since Jesus' exaltation to God's right hand, he is the one who has placed prophets in the Body of believers (1 Cor. 12:28; Eph. 4:7-11).

Although every Christian can prophesy, there is a difference between someone operating the manifestation of prophecy and someone who has

---

7. To help you better understand and bring forth the manifestation of prophecy, see Appendix E, "Examples of Prophecy in the Bible."

8. For more information on speaking in tongues and the interpretation of tongues, visit www.TruthOrTradition.com TOPIC: Manifestations. If you have never spoken in tongues and would like to, read the article titled "What is Speaking in Tongues and Why Does God Say to do it?"

the gift ministry of a prophet. The gift ministry of a prophet is covered in Appendix A.

CHAPTER FIVE
Things to Consider When Receiving a Prophecy

1. Before receiving a prophecy, it is good to learn something about it and be prepared to receive it. Prophecy is a way that you can hear from the Lord himself about his love and concern for you and about his will for your life. Your personal prophecy will mean a lot more to you if you know what prophecy is and how it works, and if you prepare your heart to receive it, evaluate it, and act on it. If you have questions about prophecy, you should ask them. Also, it can be good to have godly, trusted friends listen to your prophecy and give you their opinion—there is safety in a multitude of counselors.

2. Christians are filled with holy spirit, and have the Bible, so why would they need prophecy? Will the Lord not tell them directly what they need to know? It is always the Lord's heart to communicate with his Body, the Church. It is important to realize that personally hearing from the Lord should be the "default pattern" for every Christian. Furthermore, obeying the written Word of God and using wisdom is also vital to successful Christian living. If you are not making enough money to make ends meet, you do not need a prophet to tell you to cut back your spending or get a better paying job. That is simply the wise thing to do. Hearing from the Lord for yourself, obeying Scripture, and using wisdom are always the first things you should do in your Christian walk and life.

Nevertheless, prophecy is still important to individuals, which is why the Bible says that we are to be eager to prophesy (1 Cor. 14:39). The Lord can speak through prophecy in times when a Christian is not hearing his voice due to being new in the faith, having doubts about his life and walk, or being too emotionally involved with a situation to hear clearly. Or, there may be times when the person receiving a prophecy has thought something about a situation, but has not believed it firmly enough to act on it. In fact, people often receive in prophecy the confirmation of something they have believed, and are then able to fully put their faith in it. It is also common in prophecy that as the Lord reveals things about someone's life, that person feels a special connection to him that he did not have before.

3. Make sure you are comfortable receiving a prophecy, and with the person or persons giving it to you. Receiving a prophecy can be a great blessing, but not if you are not ready for it, feel like it is being forced upon you, or are not comfortable with the person or persons giving the prophecy. Just as prophets do not have to give a word to everyone who asks, you do not have to receive a word from someone just because he says he heard from the Lord about you. When you are ready to receive, and comfortable with the one who would speak it to you, then you are in a position to have faith that the Lord will powerfully energize the prophecy, and you will be ready to believe and act on what is spoken. Faith is a great key in any spiritual endeavor, and your faith will contribute to energizing those prophesying to you.

People who have given many words of personal prophecy testify that when the person receiving it has desire and faith, then the prophecy flows very easily—the prophetic word is almost pulled out of them. In contrast, if someone comes for prophecy whose heart is not ready to receive it, then many times giving the prophecy becomes much more difficult. If you are not comfortable about receiving a prophecy, you should want to identify why not, and you should not receive a prophecy until you are ready to receive it with faith.

4. The manifestation of prophecy is primarily to build up a person in his Christian walk and help establish his relationship with God and the Lord Jesus. The manifestation of prophecy is for "…edification, and exhortation, and comfort" (1 Cor. 14:3b-KJV). Furthermore, when a person receives a prophecy, "…the secrets of his heart will be laid bare…" (1 Cor. 14:25a). It is very important to understand that the manifestation of prophecy is not primarily designed to reveal detailed information about the future, or give specific guidance about what a person should do in a specific situation. Although this kind of specific information can occasionally be given in the manifestation of prophecy, it is usually given by those people in the Church who have the ministry of a prophet.[1]

God is very concerned about the quality of each Christian's walk with Him. Sadly, many Christians have never really had a "personal experience" with God. We talk about it, preach about it, and write about it, but the fact is that many Christians are in the same place Job was some 4,000 years ago: the best they can say is, "My ears had heard of you…" (Job 42:5a). The manifestation of prophecy, by revealing the secrets of the heart, is designed by God to bring the person to the place that he will "…fall down and worship God, exclaiming, 'God is really among you!'" (1 Cor. 14:25b). Often a prophecy will have details about a person's life that, when revealed, help him believe that the Lord knows and understands him personally, and cares for him.

> People who have given many words of personal prophecy testify that when the person receiving it has desire and faith, then the prophecy flows very easily.

When Job experienced God for himself (Job 38:1- 42:6), there was a profound change in his life. Like many others, he had heard about God for years, but never had a "personal encounter." When he did, his life changed. Many Christians testify that their lives were changed in important ways after they received a prophecy revealing to them that God really did know them and what they were going through in life, and had been with them in tough times and good times. Experience teaches us that usually when a person receives a prophecy, he feels very connected to the Lord. However, not all prophecy comes with a warm, fuzzy feeling. It sometimes happens when the Lord exhorts a person to do better in something that he may have feelings of guilt or sadness. Appropriate feelings of guilt or sadness can bring a person to make changes in his life that are positive and godly (2 Cor. 7:8-11).

The manifestation of prophecy is for "…edification, and exhortation, and comfort" (1 Cor. 14:3b-KJV). The NIV reads, "…strengthening, encouragement, and comfort." The word "exhortation" in the KJV is

---

1. For more on the ministry of a prophet, see Appendix A.

better than "encouragement" in the NIV because it covers a wider range of what can be spoken in prophecy.[2] God does not give prophecy to condemn us, nor use it as a platform to complain about our lives. There are times, however, when prophecy will convict someone in his heart, and motivate him to change. People can ask for a prophecy knowing God loves them, wants the best for them, and will communicate in a way that will help them in their walk. The prophetic message will build them up, exhort them in their walk, and comfort their hearts.

5. Evaluate and weigh carefully what is spoken by the one prophesying. There is always a chance that inaccuracies will enter into a prophecy. The Word of God tells us to "Test everything. Hold on to the good" (1 Thess. 5:21). There are some basic ways that you can test to see if a prophecy is from the Lord. A good way to remember them is to call them "the four Ws."

A. The Word of God. Prophecy will not contradict the written Word. God is not the author of confusion, and He will never confuse believers by saying one thing in His Word and another in prophecy. If you get a prophecy that blatantly contradicts the letter or spirit of the written Word of God, do not move forward in obeying it.

B. Wisdom. The Bible tells us to love God with all our minds, and He is the author of wisdom, which is to be a primary guide for our lives. The words "wise" and "wisdom" occur well over 100 times in Proverbs alone. God expects us to use wisdom to know right from wrong. If you receive a prophecy directing you to do something you consider unwise or that is somehow suspicious to you, get the counsel of others before proceeding.

C. Witness. Every Christian has the gift of holy spirit, and can hear from the Lord directly. If you receive a prophecy that is genuinely from the Lord, you should also have an inner witness that it is correct. If you have no such witness, it does not mean

---

2. See "Exhortation" in the Glossary.

that the prophecy is necessarily wrong, but it does mean that you should get the wise counsel of others before acting on it.

D. Work Out. The Lord will work hard to confirm a prophecy. If you receive a prophecy, and you do your part to see it come to pass, then you can legitimately expect it to come to pass, i.e., "work out." If it does not, then you have very good reason to think you received an erroneous word.

Because the flesh can enter into prophecy, you need to seek godly and wise counsel if you receive one you are not confident about, especially if it directs you to do something that will have an important impact on your life. If you receive a prophecy that you are not sure is true or accurate, you should not act on it immediately. Put it on the "back burner" and pray about it. Ask the Lord to speak to you in other ways to confirm or deny what you heard. For example, you might pray for a wide open door that is obvious, or you may pray to hear the same thing from another source. When we get the true word of the Lord and act upon it, there is great blessing for us.

6. Prophecy is not "the Word of God." The written Word of God is "God-breathed" (2 Tim. 3:16). Every syllable in the original is perfect. That is not the case with the manifestation of prophecy. Do not fall into the trap of analyzing every syllable and preposition in your prophecy. Instead, ask, "What is the point of the message; what is the Lord saying?" As one prophet has said, "It is important to get the 'take home' message." A great example of this is in the book of Acts, where Agabus, a seasoned prophet of God, gave Paul a word not to go to Jerusalem.

Acts 21:10-12
(10) After we had been there a number of days, a prophet named Agabus came down from Judea.
(11) Coming over to us, he took Paul's belt, tied his own hands and feet with it and said, "The Holy Spirit says, 'In this way the Jews of Jerusalem will **bind the owner of this belt and will hand him over to the Gentiles**.'"

(12) When we heard this, we and the people there pleaded with Paul not to go up to Jerusalem.

Paul was so determined to go to Jerusalem that he ignored what the Lord spoke through prophecy. What happened when he got there, however, was not exactly what Agabus had said. If you read the record in Acts 21:30-33, you will see that, instead of capturing Paul and binding him and handing him over to the Romans, the Jews were in the middle of beating him to death when the Romans broke in and saved him. However, thinking Paul to be some kind of criminal, the Romans arrested him. He spent the next two years in jail in Israel, and then was taken as a prisoner to Rome. Agabus' prophecy was not fulfilled "letter perfect." But there is no doubt that the gist, the "take home message," of the prophecy was correct: Paul should not have gone to Jerusalem. When he did, he was rejected by the Jews and ended up in Roman chains.

When you receive a prophecy, do not get hung up on the details and miss the big picture. Remember to ask, "What is the point the Lord is making?"

7. Be careful not to quickly reject a prophecy that does not seem right to you. Although you should hold in abeyance a prophecy you are not sure is accurate, always be cautious about totally rejecting prophecy from a prophet who has been tested and proved, even if it does not seem correct. As humans, we have strong feelings and emotions, and the way we were taught or the way we have done something in the past can have a powerful influence on us. A prophecy that seems to go against what we are used to may seem "wrong" to us even when it is actually biblically and ethically correct.

Imagine a Christian who has always worn a crucifix for good luck and personal protection receiving a prophecy that the Lord wanted him to rely on the Lord and not on such objects. He might tend to reject the words of the prophet as absurd. Or imagine a group of people who believe water baptism is necessary for salvation hearing a man prophesy to a Christian who had never been water baptized, stating that the Lord fully accepts him. The people listening might be tempted to call the prophet a false prophet, when actually he is absolutely correct.

What you believe is not necessarily true, even if you believe it very strongly. If you hear something that contradicts what you have always believed or practiced, you may have a strong emotional reaction, which, as real and powerful as it is, is not the voice of the Lord. As with so many other things in life, there is no formula that will tell you if the prophet is correct and your thoughts are wrong, or vice versa. As always, we need to rely on the written Word, wisdom, the counsel of others, and the direction of the Lord via his gift of holy spirit.

8. Prophecy can be about gifts and callings that have not yet manifested themselves. Occasionally, a prophecy will address something that the Lord sees in the future, which the person receiving the prophecy is not yet aware of. The prophecy of Samuel to David about being the king of Israel is a clear example (1 Sam. 16:13). There is no evidence that David had ever even thought about being king, especially in a culture where kingship followed family lines. Furthermore, it was approximately 15 years after Samuel anointed David king that he actually saw the prophecy fulfilled. So if you receive a prophecy that does not come to pass in a short time, do not be too hasty to call it a false prophecy. When you receive a prophecy, and especially if it involves something that will be fulfilled in the future, have patience and faith that it will be fulfilled. Do not be quick to give up on the Lord. Walk in patience and faithful expectation that what he has said will indeed come to pass in your life.

9. Just because God does not mention a sin does not mean it is okay with Him. Due to the fallen nature of man, people will sometimes knowingly or unknowingly try to justify their sin, and may use prophecy to do so. Someone who is engaged in a sinful activity may ask to receive a prophecy but be thinking, "If the Lord does not mention my doing (whatever), then it must be okay with him. After all, if it were that bad he would say something." This is false logic. The Lord expects you to live a godly life. You do not expect him to tell you by revelation to stop at a red light or to return a wallet you found on the street. What you can easily know from the Word, experience, and your senses, the Lord expects you to know and act on.

It is the same with sin in your life. If you are sinning, stop. Do not expect the Lord to speak about something that is clear in the Bible and/or obvious to you. The written Word is the standard for godly behavior.

10. When you receive an accurate prophecy, obey it. Prophecy is not a toy, nor is it a test to prove that God knows us or loves us. Neither is it to prove the person giving the prophecy is "right on" and can discover some hidden thing. When done properly, prophecy is God or His Son, Jesus, speaking to you through the mouth of the one giving the prophecy. When accurate, prophecy is as valid as if Jesus were standing there talking to you. Because of that, when you ask for a prophecy, make sure that you have the proper attitude about it and are ready to obey it. As you prepare yourself to receive a prophecy, think about what your attitude would be if, instead of going to someone manifesting the spirit, you were going to sit at the feet of the Lord Jesus and hear what he had to say to you. We want to honor the Lord by giving his word the attention it deserves. We should test them to be sure they are the words of the Lord, but if they are, then we need to give heed to them.

1 Thessalonians 5:20 and 21 (NASB)
(20) do not despise prophetic utterances.
(21) But examine everything *carefully*; hold fast to that which is good;

The word "despise" in verse 20 is *exoutheneo*, which means to despise or treat with scorn, and therefore "to reject with scorn."[3] If you ask for a prophecy and receive one you believe to be accurate, but do not obey it, you are rejecting it and are sinning. In the Old Testament, if someone came to the priests for information but after getting it decided not to obey what they said, he was put to death (Deut. 17:8-13). Obviously, we do not put people to death today if they ignore words of prophecy, but you

---

3. Spiros Zodhiates, *The Complete Word Study Dictionary* (AMG Publishers, Chattanooga, TN, 1992), p. 606.

can be sure that the Lord gets upset if you go to him for a prophecy and then ignore it. James 4:17 says, "Anyone, then, who knows the good he ought to do and doesn't do it, sins."

The Lord wants to be treated the same way we do. If someone comes to you and asks for information and then ignores what you said, you would be upset. The same is true of the Lord. If you ask for a prophecy, act on it. Remember the scripture that says, "…From everyone who has been given much, much will be demanded; and from the one who has been entrusted with much, much more will be asked" (Luke 12:48b). When you are given a prophecy, you are being given "much," and the Lord requires your obedience in return.

11. We must play our part in order to have prophecy come to pass. It is vital to realize that even accurate prophecies about the future do not usually come to pass automatically. We have to do something in order for them to be fulfilled. We must pray, obey, and walk in godly wisdom. This is true for revelation we receive directly from the Lord and for prophecy spoken to us. When prophecies are not fulfilled quickly, discouragement, disillusionment, and disbelief can enter our heads and hearts, and we must work hard to fight them off, continuing to have faith in the prophecy. Abraham is a great example to us because when God gave him the revelation he would have a child, "…he did not waver through unbelief regarding the promise of God, but was strengthened in his faith and gave glory to God" (Rom. 4:20). Abraham continued to have faith during the 30 years between the time God gave him the promise and when it was finally fulfilled by the birth of Isaac.

Abraham's experience, though extreme, is not unique. David was a teenager when Samuel anointed him king, but it was not until he was 30 years old when all the tribes of Israel got together, officially recognized his kingship, anointed him, and installed him as king (2 Sam. 5:3 and 4). During those years between the promise and the fulfillment of his kingship, David was faithful to the promise of God, and led the people God gave him.

Like faith, prayer is very important in seeing prophecies come to pass. Daniel is known for his deep prayer life. When he read the prophecy of Jeremiah that the desolation of Israel would be 70 years (Dan. 9:2), his response was not, "Oh well, I'll sit back, count the years, and the prophecy will automatically come to pass." Daniel knew that a lot had to happen for the prophecy to be fulfilled, and that time was short. The Bible records one of the things he did: "So I turned to the Lord God and pleaded with him in prayer and petition, in fasting, and in sackcloth and ashes" (Dan. 9:3). We need to pray that what has been revealed in prophecy will come to pass.

There are times when we must work very hard in order for a specific prophecy to come to pass. When God told the Israelites He would give them the Promised Land, they knew they had to fight battle after battle to have that prophecy come true. When a prophet anointed Jehu king of Israel, Jehu knew he had a lot of work to do to make that prophecy come to pass, especially since there already was a king of Israel that he would have to depose. He got to work immediately, and planned his strategy for success (2 Kings 9:1-14).

12. Focus on your walk, your calling, and your prophecy. An individual's personal prophecy is the Lord speaking to him via a Christian operating the manifestation of prophecy. This is a great honor and privilege, and should be a great source of blessing, inspiration, and sometimes challenging exhortation. Occasionally, when someone gets a personal prophecy, instead of using it to improve himself and move ahead with the Lord, he sits and pouts and wishes that the Lord had said other things to him than what was actually said. Such behavior can be especially defeating if the person then listens to a prophecy that someone else received and wishes that he had the other person's prophecy instead of the one he received, eventually becoming mentally defeated and stuck in the belief that he is no good or the Lord simply has no use for him.

There is a time for wishing and wanting something: it is when you are not walking up to your potential and you know it. That is the time to thank the Lord for the chance to live another day, make resolutions to do better, and make plans to live a more godly lifestyle. You may even want to enlist the aide of friends to help you become a more powerful and effective child of God. It is not helpful to sit and mope about what you do not have. The Lord wants us all to live at our full potential, and he stretches us in our faith and our walk. If you receive a prophecy that blesses you and excites you, wonderful! Walk out on what the Lord has revealed. If you receive a prophecy that reveals you have room to grow in your life, thank the Lord for his honesty and get about the task of growing and maturing in your Christian life. If you have fallen down or feel weak in your walk, get up and get going. The Lord will be with you to love you, support you, and bless you, but you are the one who must get up and get going. Proverbs 24:16a says, "for though a righteous man falls seven times, he rises again...."

13. It is helpful to record personal prophecies. It is a very good idea to have your personal prophecy recorded (and perhaps even written out at a later time). The primary reason for this is that we are not used to remembering what is said to us, and forget many details, especially over time. Another reason is that you may hear something that catches your attention and causes you to miss other things that are said. A third reason is that often we mishear what was actually said. Having a recording gives us the ability to go back and listen to what was said. Remember, a word or phrase may have several applications. Prophetic language is often figurative and uses analogies, similes, metaphors, etc.

> There are times when we must work very hard in order for a specific prophecy to come to pass.

Sometimes going back over what was said reveals things that were missed or misunderstood. Also, it may be helpful to write the prophecies out so that they can be easily reviewed and prayed over. Many people keep a binder with prayer goals and prophecies to help them have a vision for their future and enable them to see more clearly when God works in their life.

14. Over time, a "prophetic picture" will develop from your prophecies. If you are receiving prophecies that are accurate, after a while you will begin to notice that together they paint a cohesive picture.

That makes perfect sense because your gifts and callings do not change day to day. Circumstances may change, the seasons of your life may change, but your calling and ministry do not. For example, if you have evangelistic tendencies, then the Lord will be exhorting you to talk to people and work on outreach at whatever stage of life you are in. If you tend to be pastoral, the Lord will be encouraging you to help the downcast and broken people around you no matter what you are involved with in your life. Building a prophetic picture over time can help you recognize the overall will of the Lord for your life.

CHAPTER SIX
Things to Know When Giving a Prophecy

1. A word of caution: practice holy living before giving prophecy. Please, do not get involved with prophetic ministry if you are engaged in and practicing sinful behavior in your personal life. The prophet is one who speaks for God, and it can be very harmful to the one giving the prophecy as well as the one receiving it if the person who speaks in the name of God is actually voicing his or her personal opinion or demonic information (Jer. 23). The life of the one who speaks for God should be an example of holiness, obedience, and service. Sin gives the Enemy access to your life (which he may or may not take advantage of), and the danger of not giving a "pure word" of prophecy increases dramatically. For your sake and the sake of those you would speak to, practice holy living before practicing prophecy.

2. The manifestation of prophecy is for edification, exhortation, and comfort. When a Christian brings forth the manifestation of prophecy, it will, with rare exception, be for edification, exhortation, and comfort (1 Cor. 14:3-KJV). Generally, God will give a prophetic message that involves stern reproof via a person with the gift ministry of a prophet. On the other hand, "edification" and "exhortation" can contain some very strong words. We know from John 15 that edification, which means "building up" (the NIV translates it as "strengthening"), often involves pruning.

John 15:1 and 2
(1) I am the true vine, and my Father is the gardener.
(2) He cuts off every branch in me that bears no fruit, while every branch that does bear fruit he prunes so that it will be even more fruitful.

Pruning can be painful, and sometimes what the Lord says to a person in prophecy can be uncomfortable. However, remember that the purpose of pruning is to produce a stronger vine. No Christian who loves the Lord wants to hear only what the Lord is pleased about in his life. We should all want to know what the Lord really wants from us so we can walk in the center of his will. If that involves some pruning, then so be it. It is important to know, however, that there will never be any condemnation in the manifestation of prophecy. Nor will any sins that have been confessed and forgiven be brought up.

Just as the process of building someone up and strengthening him can involve some painful words, so can "exhortation." The individual who never prays publicly might, for example, be exhorted or encouraged to pray in his church. Hearing that exhortation from the Lord might make him very uncomfortable, but ultimately it will be a great blessing. Another example of an exhortation that might make a person uncomfortable would be exhorting someone who keeps his faith private to learn to share it with others. The individual who received that word might be very challenged at the thought of telling people about the Lord, and might become very uncomfortable. Yet that exhortation would be the very thing he needed in order to grow in his spiritual life, something he probably wanted to do anyway.

Although the manifestation of prophecy is also for "comfort," it is wrong to think that every time an accurate prophecy is delivered, the person who receives it will walk away with a warm, fuzzy feeling. On the other hand, there is no comfort more wonderful than a prophetic word of comfort spoken to a broken heart or to someone under a lot of pressure or stress. The Lord knows how to say exactly the right thing to comfort those who are downcast, and many prophecies are words of comfort.

3. Your relationship with the Lord is essential. All revelation is either due to the individual's relationship with the Lord or due to the Lord's purposes. There is great value in having a loving and godly walk with the Lord, now and in the age to come. People who have a wonderful personal relationship with the Lord, are obedient to him, and have his interests at heart, generally receive more revelation than people who are disobedient and/or interested only in their own agendas.

There are times, however, when God will give revelation because it suits His agenda or to show His love and grace. There are many examples of this in the Old Testament. 1 Kings 13:21 and 22 contains an example of a prophet who, although a liar, received a powerful revelation because God wanted His message delivered. It is wrong to think that just because you received a powerful revelation, your doctrine is correct, or that you are walking in the center of God's will. God gave the written Word for doctrine, reproof, correction, and instruction in right living (2 Tim. 3:16), and when we obey it, then we are in the center of His will.

> There is great value in having a loving and godly walk with the Lord, now and in the age to come.

When it comes to the manifestation of prophecy, it is important to obey the Word of God and do your best to live a godly lifestyle. The revelation you receive will generally be clearer and more abundant, and your prophecy will have a greater effect and be more of a blessing.

4. Your love for people is important. The manifestation of prophecy exists because God loves His people. He does not provide prophecy so that people who prophesy proficiently are elevated in their own eyes and in the eyes of other people. If you seem to lack power in your ministry and energizing in your manifestations, do a heart-check on your motives and on the quality and quantity of your love for others. God energizes people who love others and are willing to do what it takes to bless them.

Scripture tells us that today, in the Grace Administration, what really matters to God is "...faith expressing itself through love" (Gal. 5:6). Many of the miracles of Christ were energized because of his love and compassion for people, which inspired healing (Matt. 14:14), the miracle of multiplying food (Matt. 15:29-38), giving sight to the blind (Matt. 20:34), cleansing lepers (Mark 1:41), teaching (Mark 6:34), raising the dead (Luke 7:13-15-KJV), and more. The best-known Bible verse in the world tells us that God gave His Son because He "loved the world" (John 3:16).

When a person comes to you to receive a prophecy, ask the Lord to help you see that individual as he sees him, and look on him with the love and compassion that Jesus would have if he were the one giving the prophecy.

5. Some Christians are better at prophecy than others. This is true even among men and women with the gift ministry of a prophet. The Word says, "…If a man's gift is prophesying, let him use it in proportion to his faith" (Rom. 12:6b). This does not mean that if you are not comfortable with prophecy you should stop. It means that we all need to work to increase our faith and ability to do what God wants us to do. God says that each Christian should seek to excel in the building up of the Church, which prophecy certainly does (1 Cor. 14:12).

6. Practice the manifestations much in your life. If you desire to become proficient in prophecy, prophesy often. If there are not formal occasions available, prophetic prayer (which is covered later) is a wonderful way to increase your proficiency in prophecy. Giving an accurate prophecy to a church congregation is important training for giving an accurate prophecy to an individual. Also, when time for the manifestations of speaking in tongues, the interpretation of tongues, and prophecy is made available in a church meeting, take advantage of the opportunity.

Hebrews 5:14 (NASB) speaks of the value of practice: "But solid food is for the mature, who because of practice have their senses trained to discern good and evil." Prophesying and then getting feedback from others about it, as well as about the way you express the information, helps you to be able to discern "good" (the voice of the Lord) from "evil" (other thoughts).

7. You may get part, or all, of the information you prophesy before you speak. A revelation message from the Lord may either be given to you in part or in whole before you speak it, or it may come as you are in the act of speaking. A clear example of prophecy coming in total as revelation to the prophet first, and being spoken at a later time, occurs in 2 Samuel 7:4-17. God gave Nathan the prophet a complete message about David's son building the Temple the night before Nathan spoke it to David. Before Nathan spoke the message he received, it was revelation. Later, when he spoke it, it was then prophecy.

While some prophecy is given by the Lord as revelation before it is spoken, other prophecy comes out as a "flow." In the case of a "prophetic flow," the prophet does not know the words of the prophecy until he or she actually speaks them.[1] In 1 Kings 13:21 and 22 an old prophet gave a prophecy that was spoken as a prophetic flow. Experience teaches us that the manifestation of prophecy often comes as a flow, instead of being given to the one prophesying as an intact message before it is ever spoken. Many times, however, prophecy is a blend. It can start as a revelation given before it is spoken,

> If you desire to become proficient in prophecy, prophesy often.

and then become a flow as it is being spoken. In these cases the Lord reveals a piece of information and the need to speak it forth. Then, as the person starts to speak, the Lord gives more information which the person prophesying speaks forth as he is receiving it.

8. Become aware of how the Lord works with you. The Lord reveals things to different people in different ways. Revelation may come before you deliver the prophecy, or it may come as you deliver it, or it may be a combination of the two. You may get a vision, hear something, smell something, get a taste, feel something, or just know the information.[2] The Lord treats everyone as an individual, so each person will "hear" from him in a way uniquely suited to him.

When you are learning to prophesy, be open to all the ways the Lord

---

1. This is also how speaking in tongues works. The language flows out as the person speaks. There are similarities between manifesting prophecy or speaking in tongues and the way we all speak in our native language. Nobody thinks of every word he is going to say before he says it. He speaks, and the sentence forms as he speaks it. God designed us to be verbal creatures, with speech as a primary means of communication. It makes sense that there would be similarities between speaking in our native tongue, speaking prophetically, and speaking in tongues.

2. For more on this, see Appendix D, "Revelation: What It Is and How It Is Received."

can speak, and learn how he works with you. Spend some time with seasoned prophets and get their insights about what you are learning. The prophet Samuel established a school of the prophets, and part of that was for mutual learning. If you get a message that comes to you word by word, then deliver it that way. If you tend to get pictures and impressions, learn how to accurately deliver the message that the Lord is giving you, in love, and with meekness. It is important to remember that the Lord loves you as much as he loves the person to whom you will prophesy, and he will use the opportunity of your prophesying to strengthen his relationship with you. Do not think of yourself as "just a mouthpiece" for the Lord to speak to his people. Instead, use your time in prophecy to add to your knowledge of the Lord.

Learning to deliver the message the Lord gives you accurately and with love almost always takes time. Very rarely will the revelation from the Lord be completely crystal clear. Usually there is a picture, impression, or thought that is not totally clear. The person seasoned in prophecy learns over time what the Lord is communicating, and speaks with love and wisdom.

9. The prophecy that the person speaks is under his control. Scripture states, "The spirits of prophets are subject to the control of prophets" (1 Cor. 14:32). There are many facets to applying this scripture, and we will examine a couple of them. The first and most direct is that a person operating the manifestation of holy spirit is in complete control. He is not "taken over" in any sense. God never "possesses" or takes control of people the way demons do.

The people of the New Testament world were accustomed to "prophets" who were controlled by spirits (we, as Bible-believing Christians, recognize these "spirits" are demons). The Greek oracles, the most famous of which was the oracle at Delphi, were priests and priestesses through whom the "gods" spoke.[3]

---

3. The word "oracle" is used in several different ways. It can refer to the place where the gods spoke, the message that they spoke, or the person through whom they spoke.

Many mediums get their information from the spirit world while in a "trance state" during which they are taken over by demons. Many pagan religions have ceremonies in which the "god" enters the person's body and controls him. If someone is "taken over" and is not in control of himself when prophesying, that person is not manifesting prophecy from the true God. God never controls Christians for prophecy or any other manifestation. That means if Christians are going to manifest the holy spirit, they must want to manifest, and learn how to do it.

Not only does God never want evil or demonic sources to be part of Christian worship services, He wants to avoid even the appearance of evil. God never wants people to be afraid of speaking in tongues or prophecy, or to confuse them with demonic practices, so He asks believers to act in an orderly manner so that the manifestations of holy spirit are never confused with demonic control. For example, He warns people about what will happen if the congregation all speaks in tongues at one time.

1 Corinthians 14:23 (KJV)
If therefore the whole church be come together into one place, and all speak with tongues, and there come in *those that are* unlearned, or unbelievers, will they not say that ye are **mad?**

1 Corinthians 14:23
So if the whole church comes together and everyone speaks in tongues, and some who do not understand or some unbelievers come in, will they not say that you are **out of your mind?**

The translations "mad" and "out of your mind" are the translators' attempt to represent the Greek text in this context of public worship, which, unfortunately, cannot be easily done in English. In the Greek pagan worship, it occasionally happened that the devotees were taken over by demons and acted in a frenzied, frantic, raving manner.[4] The New

---

4. Many cultures have religious services in which people are taken over by demons, and often it is obvious to onlookers that they are. A good book documenting this in Haitian culture is *Strange Altars* by Marcus Bach (The Bobs-Merrill Company, Inc., Indianapolis, 1952).

Testament scholar, C. K. Barrett, writes:

> "*You are mad*...does not mean, You are suffering from mental disease, but You are possessed..."[5]

God wants to prevent confusion in Christian fellowships. He never wants people who attend church to think that the congregation has been taken over by demons and gone into a religious frenzy. He makes it clear that what is done in the service "...must be done for the strengthening of the church" (1 Cor. 14:26b). "...God is not a God of disorder..." (1 Cor. 14:33a), and "...everything should be done in a fitting and orderly way" (1 Cor. 14:40). God gave us control over our minds, bodies, and the holy spirit inside us, and gave us instructions as to how to manifest holy spirit properly. Now He expects us to obey and use the control He gave us to bless others by properly operating speaking in tongues, the interpretation of tongues, and prophecy.

Another important aspect of being in control of your prophecy is that you are in control of how you deliver the message. There are times when the Lord will give you a very specific, word-for-word message, and even say when to deliver it. There are other times when there will be a flow of words as you speak. However, many times you get only a picture, an impression, a word, or a phrase. At that point it is up to you to bring forth that message in a way that flows with God's heart and His written Word. If you are in a group of people, and the Lord tells you something that you know is very private and would be hurtful if made public, you do not have to blurt it out right then and there. It is your responsibility to use wisdom.

Remember, the manifestation of prophecy is for edification, exhortation, and comfort. An extreme example of not using wisdom might be: someone is prophesying and the Lord shows him a picture

---

5. C. K. Barrett, *Black's New Testament Commentary: The First Epistle to the Corinthians* (Hendrickson Publishers, Peabody, MA, 1968), p. 326. The Greek word can also mean "out of your mind," but in the context of a worship service, the meaning of religious frenzy due to a demon is meant.

of a pornographic magazine, at which point he blurts out, "The Lord just showed me the filthy pornography you look at. You are sinning and the Lord commands you to stop." It is hard to see how that message would be edifying or exhorting even if it were based on fact. Galatians tells us to have a spirit of meekness when we work with others (Gal. 6:1-KJV). Timothy tells us that the minister must be gentle (1 Tim. 3:3). The same message can be delivered in this way: "The Lord sees the things you are casting your eyes on which are not good or good for you, and he reminds you that he wants you to focus on the things of God. He will be able to bless you more completely when you do."

When you first hear this rendition, you may think, "That prophecy was watered down. How could anyone hearing that even know it was about pornography? Are we not to speak what the Lord gives us?" Yes, but we must use wisdom in how we present a message, particularly if it is in a public setting. If the Lord really inspired you to give a more direct word of reproof, make sure that it is given privately so that it will not embarrass the one receiving it. Also, over time you will see that the same Lord who is at work in you to give the prophecy is at work in the one receiving it to quicken his understanding. The principle of speaking the truth in a manner that is gracious and easily entreated has been practiced for years in ministries that prophesy regularly, with excellent results. Remember, you are to deliver the words of the Lord with love. There are times when

> Learning to deliver the message the Lord gives you accurately and with love almost always takes time. Very rarely will the revelation from the Lord be completely crystal clear.

the Lord wants to deliver a message with a sterner tone, and he will let you know when that is. Usually messages containing what is called "a hard word" are delivered by those who are very seasoned in prophetic ministry, and especially by those called as prophets.

Another thing to be aware of is that the Lord will communicate to you as an individual in ways that may make sense to you but not to others. If you prophesy a lot, those ways will become clearer and clearer to you.

In the example above with the magazine, it may well be that the Lord is simply communicating to you exactly what the second message said: that the person is casting his eyes in places they should not be. Another example might be if the Lord gave you a picture of a dog, and in the past you had received such pictures with an inspirational word that the person was a faithful friend. As you mature, the Lord may give you the picture without the inspiration, but you would have seen it before and would now realize that he is communicating to you that the person is faithful, a message which you could state without mentioning the picture.

10. When you speak prophetically, give only the Lord's message. The prophet Balaam made a wonderful statement about prophecy: "…I cannot go beyond the word of the LORD my God, to do less or more" (Num. 22:18b-KJV). When the Lord gives you a prophecy for someone, he expects you to deliver that word and nothing more, and that requires great discipline. Some people who receive a word talk on and on, expounding their ideas about what the Lord has revealed to them, but the disciplined believer learns what the Lord is speaking and delivers only that message. If the person prophesying has some thoughts to add, and if there is time and opportunity, he might say, "I have some ideas and insights that might be a blessing, and I can talk with you about them later."

Not only should you not add to the words of the Lord, do not take away from them either. It is a wonderful privilege to be able to bring the Lord's word to his Church, and we need to speak what he says to us. Sometimes he will show you something that seems so totally contrary to what you see by your senses that you hesitate in bringing forth the word of the Lord. The Christian who is seasoned in the operation of the manifestation of prophecy learns to hear the voice of the Lord and is committed to bringing forth his message.

In giving a prophetic message from the Lord, pray to get the "tone" of the message from the Lord and be faithful to deliver that tone. For example, if the Lord is giving a very warm and winning message of love, do not deliver it in a deadpan voice, but try to carry the meaning in tone as well as words. Similarly, when giving a strong word of exhortation, deliver it with the force the Lord is giving you, and do not water down the message by giving it in a tone that lets the person receiving the prophecy "off the hook." When you get a prophetic message, ask how the Lord would say it if he were there in person, and then say it that way.

A person prophesying must be aware that there are times when the Lord will give him an image or message that communicates to him but would not communicate well to the one being prophesied to if spoken verbatim. In that case, the one giving the prophecy must know to put the message into a form that the one receiving the prophecy can understand. This is explained more clearly in Appendix A, "The Gift Ministry of a Prophet."

11. Share what the Lord shows you even if you do not understand it. There will be times when the Lord gives you a picture, a word, a verse, or a little piece of information that does not make any sense to you. This may be when he does not want you to know the situation and wants to communicate only to the one receiving the prophecy. As a person becomes seasoned in prophecy, he learns when to stop asking the Lord for more on the subject. Simply tell the person what you received. "The Lord gave me a picture of a little house in the woods surrounded by a white picket fence. That is all I got from him." Or, "The Lord gave me the word 'lighthouse.' Nothing else, just that word." Do not guess at the meanings of the pictures or words. If the meaning is there, say it; if it is not, just speak what was given to you.

12. Do not claim to be speaking for the Lord unless you are confident you are. Occasionally you will have a very strong impression about something in the life of a person you are prophesying to but, for various reasons, you are not sure it is the Lord. Perhaps you know the person very well and you are not sure whether what you are thinking is from the Lord or your mind. If you have an impression but not a clear word, instead of saying, "The Lord says to you," you should say something such as, "I have the impression that," or "I believe the Lord is showing me that," or some similar phrase that does not state that what you are giving is unquestionably revelation from the Lord. In fact, due to the fallible nature of our flesh, many prophets avoid saying "The Lord says…" or other definite statements to that effect unless they are very clear on the revelation they are receiving. If what you are saying is truly from the Lord, the person receiving the prophecy will come to know it, whether or not you say it is from the Lord.[6]

13. Do not hold back in prophecy just because you know the person will not like what you say. Many prophets assert that the most common problem in giving a prophecy is "men pleasing." It is vital to prepare your heart to speak what the Lord gives you, period. Sometimes you may think the person you are giving a word to will be offended by what you are going to bring forth. If they are, they may even say things such as, "You did not really hear from the Lord," or "You were out to get me," or even "You are an accuser of the brethren!" Every Christian who does personal prophecy "steps into the ring" of the spiritual battle. You must be mature enough in the Lord that you are ready to do battle if need be. Your job is to deliver the message from the Lord. Usually, the one receiving the prophecy feels blessed, but sometimes he does not.

For example, someone who thinks he is ready to be launched into public ministry, when in fact he has never dealt with his own pride and ego, may hear a prophecy such as: "The Lord loves you very much and is preparing you to minister to his people. He is calling you to a time of training and learning, a time of preparation and study. He will surround you with men from whom you can learn, and will begin to give you knowledge in areas that are still unknown to you." For most people that would be a wonderful prophecy and they would be very blessed. But if the person came expecting to get a prophecy proclaiming that he was to step out and publicly lead God's people, he might be hurt and possibly angry.

---

6. Many people try to affirm their relationship with the Lord to others by regularly saying, "The Lord told me to do such-and-such," or, "The Lord told me to say such-and-such." Generally, if the Lord directs a person to say or do something, that revelation is between the person and the Lord, and should stay that way. That the person got revelation will become obvious to others in time. Each person should desire to develop a personal relationship with the Lord that has an element of privacy and intimacy to it.

He might claim it was not from God and the one who gave the prophecy was out to destroy his ministry. This can be very hard to deal with. No one likes to see people angry or disappointed, and few of us want to be the object of scorn, or be talked about behind our backs, as sometimes happens when someone does not like a prophecy. Nevertheless, we are to please the Lord, not men.

Jesus Christ often found himself in situations where some people were blessed and others were very upset by what he said. He occasionally used the phrase, "He who has ears to hear, let him hear" (Matt. 11:15-NASB). The point is this: the job of the one prophesying is to bring the message that the Lord gives him. It is up to people to prepare their hearts and lives to be able to receive that message. If they do not, we do not "tailor make" a prophecy in order to make them happy.

14. How do you know that what you are getting is from the Lord? Sometimes you will not be sure whether you have gotten information from the Lord or from your mind. Before you prophesy, it is always vital to keep yourself free of judgments and be confident that your motives are pure. This is not something you can do right then and there, but rather is the result of working hard to be godly, honest, pure, free from anger and bitterness—in a word, being Christ-like in your life. You may not be perfect, but you should know whether you have any sin problems and if you are dealing with them in a godly and honest manner.

If you are prophesying in a team situation and are not sure the word you seem to have is from the Lord, but it is something the Lord wants communicated, usually someone else will speak it. At that point you can be sure it was the Lord and not your mind, and the experience will add to your knowledge of how he speaks to you. Another thing you can do is simply be honest with the person you are prophesying to and tell him that you have an impression but are not sure if it is you or the Lord, and would they mind your sharing it anyway. If they agree, after you do, you can ask them if they thought it was from the Lord. Listening to others is a wonderful way to learn.

It may be that after you give a prophecy you find out it was not from the Lord, but from your mind. What do you do when you make a mistake? You apologize to the person to whom you gave the prophecy, ask the Lord to forgive you, and keep moving forward. There is no shame in making an honest mistake, and the possibility of making one emphasizes the need for prophesying as part of a team.

15. It is unwise to say certain things. A good guideline to stick by in the manifestation of prophecy, and one that is used in many prophetic circles, is: "Do not tell people to marry, bury, buy, sell, or move geographically." There are some things that the Lord may give you insight about that are not necessarily wise to affirm as the word of the Lord. For example, you may know that the person you are prophesying to is dating someone, and you may think you have a revelation from the Lord that he is telling you that he will bless the two of them if they decide to marry. It is still not wise to say anything about it. Even though you feel strongly about the situation, you still must use wisdom in how you deal with it.

Remember, the manifestation of prophecy is for strengthening, encouragement, and comfort. Directing someone to buy or sell something, or to move from one location to another, or to marry someone should be done only on the basis of absolutely clear revelation, and even then it should have confirmation by others. However, if you are a called prophet or seasoned in prophecy, then speak what you believe the Lord gave you. Isaiah told Hezekiah he was about to die (2 Kings 20:1); when David was running from Saul he sought the Lord about moving and was given guidance about it (1 Sam. 22:5); and other prophets foretold the relocation of kings and even kingdoms. The seasoned prophet speaks what the Lord reveals, but if you are not a prophet, or are one but not yet seasoned in your ministry, remember that your gift of holy spirit is under your control, and it is neither wise nor godly to speak out every thought you believe the Lord gives you as if it were unquestionably from him.

16. Be brief, but cover the subject. Often in prophecy, less is more. People sometimes have a tendency in delivering a prophecy to go on and on, stating and restating what the Lord has revealed. This usually does not help, and can actually cause the person receiving the prophecy to lose focus. Also, in the written Word, when something is repeated twice it is established by God and will quickly come to pass. Do not repeat the message of the Lord over and over using different words unless he directs you to. Work on your delivery so that it is concise and accurate.

If you are a person who tends to repeat himself over and over, stating and restating the prophecy, it is good to ask yourself why that is and work on the heart issues that produce the problem. Do you lack confidence that what you said was from the Lord and so you say it over to confirm it to yourself? Do you think that if the prophecy is stated concisely that the listener will not really get the message? Do you just like the "feel" of speaking prophetically and so become long-winded? Become aware of what you are saying in your prophecy and deliver the message from the Lord clearly and concisely.

> A good guideline to stick by in the manifestation of prophecy, and one that is used in many prophetic circles, is: "Do not tell people to marry, bury, buy, sell, or move geographically."

17. Team prophecy can be a blessing. The Lord has put Christians together in a body, and each member has his own strengths and weaknesses. Beside that, each Christian brings to the table his own personal experiences, knowledge, likes and dislikes, etc. Because of that, some people tend to be especially sensitive to certain information while perhaps not being as sensitive to other things the Lord is wanting to reveal. Christians who have been part of a "prophetic team" have seen how the Lord works in each member to bring their best to the person receiving the prophecy. If you are giving a prophecy to someone, seriously consider getting one or two other believers to join you.

Another good reason for prophesying as a team is that the Lord often honors his Body by not giving the "whole pie" of prophecy to one individual. It is very often the case that one person prophesying will get just a piece of the will of the Lord, and another will be energized by the Lord to start his or her prophecy where the other left off.

The team concept is tried and true. History credits Samuel as being the first prophet to establish a "school of the prophets." It is during the lifetime of Samuel that we first see companies of prophets traveling and training together. Scriptures that show evidence of companies of prophets together for support and training include: 1 Samuel 10:5, 19:20; 2 Kings 2:3 and 5, 4:38 and 6:1.[7]

Another reason for team prophecy is that people often get energized in a wonderful and powerful way while prophesying together. There is something important and powerful that occurs when two or more people stand together in prayer and faith to bless and help others. Even Jesus sent the apostles out in groups of two. He later said, "For where two or three come together in my name, there am I with them" (Matt. 18:20).

18. It is important to properly evaluate the prophecies of others. The Bible tells prophets to weigh carefully what others are saying in their prophecies: "Two or three prophets should speak, and the others should weigh carefully what is said" (1 Cor. 14:29). The major reason to weigh carefully what others say is that, as humans, our flesh can and occasionally does get in the way of hearing the voice of the Lord, causing us to bring forth an inaccurate word. When that happens, other prophets should realize it via the spirit of God, and gently and humbly say they do not agree with what was spoken. At times like these, protecting the heart and life of the one receiving the prophecy is much more important than the feelings of the one giving it. Anyone who steps into the spiritual arena to prophesy for another person should have already obtained a level of spiritual maturity such that they would understand that they could be in error when they

---

7. Many scholars refer to what Samuel organized as a "School of the Prophets." Keil and Delitzsch write: "...there can be no doubt that these unions of the prophets arose in the time of Samuel and were called into existence by him. [The schools of the prophets] were associations formed for the purpose of mental and spiritual training, that they might exert a more powerful influence upon their contemporaries. The name 'schools of the prophets' is the one which expresses most fully the character of these associations...." C. F. Keil and F. Delitzsch, *Commentary on the Old Testament* (William B. Eerdmans Publishing Company, Grand Rapids, MI, reprinted 1975), Vol. 2, pp. 199-203.

prophesy for people, and be thankful for the loving help of others. Although 1 Corinthians 14:29 is written specifically to those with the ministry of a prophet, the love the Lord has for each person who receives a prophecy, along with the gift of holy spirit in each believer, means that any Christian present may recognize that what another has spoken is not genuine, and they should intercede for the one receiving the word.

Prophets being subject to one another protects the Church, because people can be greatly hurt by erroneous prophecy. Being subject to one another is part of the mature Christian walk, and the natural response to recognizing that at any given time, no matter how strongly anyone feels about something, he might be wrong. One of the aspects of 1 Corinthian 14:32 ("The spirits of prophets are subject to the control of prophets") is that the prophets are to support one another and the Church by being subject to each other.

It is usually the case that when a prophet receives a revelation, it will be able to be confirmed in part or in whole by other prophets (which may be as simple as other prophets getting no "check" on it, or by feeling good in general about the revelation). Sometimes the Lord is already working in other prophets, and sometimes the matter becomes confirmed to other prophets as they consider it. Nevertheless, it may happen that a prophet would receive a revelation that by its very nature had to be delivered before other prophets could be conferred, the prophet felt the need to keep the word between himself and the one receiving the prophecy, or perhaps the Lord had another reason for only giving the revelation to one prophet. In that case, as in every prophecy, the prophet must stand accountable for the word he gave. If it were later proved to be wrong, then obviously his credibility would be diminished and some kind of censure may need to be applied.

Prophecy is a mighty weapon in the Lord's arsenal, and we dare not take the teeth out of it by instituting rules and regulations that quench it, but also we need to understand the general principle by which the Lord works in his Church today. As we said, generally the Lord works in such a way that a prophetic word can be confirmed, so that confusion is not sown into the Church and a situation of "dueling prophets" does not arise that would force the Church to take sides. Generally, what the Lord says to one prophet, he will confirm to another, which is why verse 29 says prophetic words are to be weighed carefully. When prophets disagree as to whether a word is from the Lord, the proper thing to do to avoid hurting the Church is for them not to speak publicly or openly until they resolve the matter. If a prophet thinks he or she has received a word but there is some question about it, or if there are other prophets to check with, then allowing oneself to be in subjection before speaking the prophecy is always a wise practice.

It is important that anyone who is going to listen and evaluate the prophecies of others should be mature, godly, and mentally healthy. If we have a "plank" in our own eye, we are in no position to clearly see a "speck" in the eye of someone else (Matt. 7:3). Before correcting the prophecy given by someone else, we should do our best to make sure we are able to make a "right judgment" (John 7:24).

19. Keep confidentiality when giving prophecy. Seasoned prophets will tell you that one of the surest ways to stop hearing from the Lord is to "blab" to your friends what he revealed to you about someone, and then begin to gossip about the person. If the Lord reveals to you some less than flattering information about someone, and you tell your friends about it, you are sinning against the Lord and the person. Jesus Christ died for that person you just defamed, and he gave you the word he did because there is a chance the person might be delivered. If you are the type of person who struggles with confidentiality, and occasionally just cannot seem to keep a secret, then be careful getting involved with personal prophecy. Far better you should arrive at the Judgment Seat not ever having given a prophecy than get there and face the Lord after spreading harmful information. Remember, a gossip reveals secrets, but love covers a multitude of sins (Prov. 11:13, 17:9; 1 Pet. 4:8). However, taking a prophecy to other mature Christians for prayer and counsel is not gossip. The key to whether or not a communication is gossip is the motive of the heart.

20. Sometimes we need to ask permission before giving a prophecy. Many times it is appropriate and important to ask the person for whom you have a word if he would like to receive it. This might be when you are giving prophecy from the stage during a conference or church service, or giving prophecy to someone you do not know. Asking can be very helpful because it assures you that the person is ready and willing, and it honors his free will. There are times when you have a word for someone, but he or she does not want it delivered in public, for whatever reason. Asking permission allows them to voice that fact. If you do not ask, the person may become offended, in which case the effect of the prophecy is greatly reduced, and you also have to deal with his hurt feelings.

21. Do not give a prophecy to a person just because he asks; check with the Lord. If someone asks for a prophecy, ask the Lord whether it is right to give it. Scripture shows that the Lord did not answer every person who came to him. The Lord knows the hearts of all men, and if you do not feel it is his will to give a prophecy, then do not give one. Some people have unrealistic expectations of the Lord and want a prophecy every week. Others are very insecure and do not want to do anything without "hearing from the Lord about it." Others may not trust that the Lord loves them, and so they want to be assured over and over that he is "taking notice" of what they are doing. People like this are one reason why Christians who prophesy should be mature. You may have to tell someone who comes to you for a prophecy that what he really needs is pastoral counseling. Remember the example of Christ: he gave people what they needed, not necessarily what they asked for.

22. If a couple comes for prophecy, ask politely if they are married. In the United States of America (and most other countries), a couple is married before God when they are married in the eyes of the state. God exhorts us to keep the laws of the land and to set good examples for all mankind. If the couple is not married, give them individual prophecies. If a couple is living together without being married and they get a prophecy that has blessings or simply does not say anything about their need to get married, they may well assume that how they are living is okay with God. It is not, and the written Word of

God makes that clear. It is often the case that if the Bible says something plainly, the Lord will not say anything about it in a prophecy. It is the written Word, not the manifestation of prophecy, that is for doctrine, reproof, correction, and instruction in righteousness (2 Tim. 3:16), and each Christian needs to learn to live by the written Word.

23. When you are asking the Lord for prophetic insight, also ask if there is any need to minister healing and/or cast out demons. People who come for prophecy may also have other needs, such as physical healing or spiritual deliverance. If the Lord shows you a demon, walk with great wisdom. Most people will not know it is there, and if you tell them, they may have confusion, doubt, shame, guilt, or fear. Ask the Lord what he wants you to do. Did he show it to you so you could cast it out then and there, or later? Did he show it to you so you would know more about the situation and be able to recommend pastoral and deliverance counseling? Remember, you can often cast out a demon without specifically saying it is a demon. If you say by revelation, "I command Fear to leave this body in the name of Jesus Christ," the spirit still must leave even though you have not called it "the spirit of fear."

24. It is often easier to prophesy to someone you do not know. If you do not know the person to whom you are prophesying, there is less chance for your mind to interfere in what God wants you to say. When you prophesy to anyone, it is important to free yourself of judgments and opinions that can distort the word of the Lord. If you have very strong opinions about someone and/or know them very well, it is often better to let someone else give the prophecy. This is a guideline, however. There are examples in the Word of God of people prophesying to others who they knew very well. Noah, Isaac, and Jacob all prophesied over their children, and Nathan knew David very well. If you do know someone very well and give a prophecy to him, it is good advice to get another prophetic word on the situation.

25. Make sure you are physically and mentally ready to prophesy. It is sometimes difficult to prophesy when you are physically or emotionally tired, upset, distracted, hurt, etc. An example is in 2 Kings. The armies of Judah and Israel were attacking the Moabites but ran out of water. Not knowing what to do, they called the great prophet Elisha to the battleground to ask him. The king of Israel was very ungodly, and Elisha did not want to prophesy for him and was very upset about it. However, because of the presence of Jehoshaphat and the army of Judah, Elisha knew that the word of the Lord was essential if the lives of the men in the army were going to be saved. To help him get focused, he called for a musician to play to help him calm down.

2 Kings 3:13-15
(13) Elisha said to the king of Israel, "What do we have to do with each other? Go to the prophets of your father and the prophets of your mother [the prophets of Baal]." "No," the king of Israel answered, "because it was the LORD who called us three kings together to hand us over to Moab."
(14) Elisha said, "As surely as the LORD Almighty lives, whom I serve, if I did not have respect for the presence of Jehoshaphat king of Judah, I would not look at you or even notice you.
(15) But now bring me a harpist." While the harpist was playing, the hand of the LORD came upon Elisha.

Elisha did what was necessary to get to the place he could hear God. We need to follow his example. Do what it takes to get yourself to the place you can hear from the Lord. If you need a little rest, get some. If you are hungry and distracted, get something to eat and start again when you can focus. Very few situations need a word "this minute" and cannot wait a little while.

Having said the above, also remember it is certainly possible to hear from the Lord when you are tired, hungry, sick, or whatever. Many times in your life you will be called upon to minister when you are not "at your peak." The key is being disciplined enough in your life that you can still get quiet on the inside, focus, and hear what the Lord is saying. The best way to get to the point that you can minister when you are not at your best is to be faithful in your Christian walk. For example, if you are one who prays every day, you know there are days when you feel bad, or stressed, or pressed for time, or even "just do not feel like praying." However, if you are faithful to pray on those days, then you will develop the necessary skills to minister when you do not feel like it. The same goes for reading the Bible, going to church, giving, etc. If you serve God only when you feel like it and have time, then when you are not feeling like it you will have a hard time hearing from Him and ministering via prophecy.

26. There may be times when you do not seem to have anything from the Lord. This could be due to a number of reasons. You may not be able to focus for some reason; the person who wants the prophecy may have come with a request for specific information that the Lord is not going to reveal; the person may have just received a prophecy; or there may be another reason. There is no shame in saying you do not have anything from the Lord, but there is shame in guessing or saying that you have a word from the Lord when you do not. An example from the Bible of someone asking the LORD for guidance and not getting any occurs in 1 Samuel 28:6, when Saul inquired of God but did not get an answer. The word "inquired" in the Hebrew text, however, indicates that Saul did not have a pure heart when he asked. Referring to the same situation, but using a different Hebrew word (that means to inquire diligently), 1 Chronicles 10:14 says that Saul did not inquire of the LORD. Also, remember that James 1:5-7 says that anyone who asks but has doubt and will not believe the answer "…should not think that he will receive anything from the Lord." The Lord knows each man's heart, and prophecy will reflect that fact.

If you are prophesying for a person but do not get a word for him, you can always offer to pray for him. As you pray, you may find that a word from the Lord comes to you. Anyone with a lot of experience in personal prophecy will testify that many prophetic words have started out as prayer.

27. When you give a personal prophecy, it is a good idea to record it. In Chapter Five we covered some reasons for recording personal prophecy from the receiver's perspective. Recording the prophecy also protects the one prophesying. Often, someone who has received a prophecy will say, "You said such-and-such," when in fact you are quite sure you did not say that. The best way to settle that kind of dispute is to have a recording of the prophecy. This can become vitally important if someone does something rash as a result of something he thinks he heard in a prophecy. If things do not work out in his life, he may become very angry with the one who gave the prophecy. Without a recording of it, there is just no way to know who really said what.

28. Can someone ask for a prophecy about a specific situation? Although the manifestation of prophecy is for edification, exhortation, and comfort, it can easily be seen that those can apply to specific situations, and therefore it is available to get specific information via the manifestation of prophecy. However, the called prophets in the Church are the ones charged with bringing the Lord's direction to his Church, and therefore we as a Church should be encouraging the prophets to step forward and help by giving specific information. For more on this, see Appendix A: "The Gift Ministry of a Prophet."

29. Prophetic prayer is an important part of both prophecy and prayer. Both the Bible and experience show us that both prayer and prophecy are very important in a Christian's life, and that the two can be combined. That is, as we are praying, we take the time to ask the Lord if there is anything else we should pray for, and then pray for whatever we think he is showing us. Prophetic prayer is also a very non-threatening way to practice prophecy and to bless people. In prophetic prayer, ask God to show you something specific that will bless the person and let him know that He is involved in his life. If God reveals something to you, do not make a big show of it and say, "God just showed me thus and so." Just let it be part of your prayer, and pray for it as well as the other things you were praying for. The good fruit of your prayer will be evidence enough that God was working in you.

30. It can be beneficial to ask for feedback. After you give a prophecy, it is sometimes appropriate to ask the person who got the word what he thinks about it. As Christians, we are brothers and sisters in the family of God, and we are to love and take care of each other's hearts.

Prophecy can have a very powerful positive effect on people or it can disappoint or sadden them. Listen to your heart and to the spirit of God. The person who just received a word may need to process it for a while, or may need someone to talk to. It may be very important for you to ask the person how the prophecy affected him, or if there was something he was looking for that was not covered. Prophecy may uncover things in a person's life that need to be dealt with by other ministries. The person may need to learn more from the Bible, he may need pastoral counseling, or he may have difficult decisions to make that require some loving Christian support and wisdom. Prophecy is just one piece of all the things that the Lord provides for his Body, and the one giving the prophecy must be sensitive to the fact that the one receiving it may need other things as well.

APPENDIX A
The Gift Ministry of a Prophet

There is a distinct difference between the **manifestation of prophecy** and the **gift ministry of a prophet**. The subject of this book is the manifestation of prophecy, but this appendix covers some basics about the gift ministry of a prophet (sometimes referred to as "a called prophet"). Many people are familiar with the ministries of apostles, evangelists, pastors, and teachers. However, if we are to have everything that the Lord wants us to have as his Body, we must understand the ministry of the prophet and have prophets functioning in the Church.

In spite of the fact that prophets were vital to God's purposes in the Old Testament, the need for them today has been called into question because of the presence of the gift of holy spirit in every believer. On the Day of Pentecost, God began to unveil something He had hidden from mankind (and the Devil)—the Administration of God's Grace (Eph. 3:2). Today, in the Administration of Grace, the Lord Jesus Christ seals with holy spirit every person who gets born again (Eph. 1:13). That means every Christian has the ability to hear from God and prophesy (Acts 2:17 and 18, cp. 1 Cor. 14:5 and 24).

For many people, the immediate reaction to hearing that every Christian can prophesy is to think that prophets are no longer necessary. However, a more detailed study of Scripture (and indeed, the evidence of correct practice in the Church) reveals that is not the case. For example, Ephesians 4:11 says that the Lord has placed prophets in the Church along with the other ministries of apostles, evangelists, pastors, and teachers. Furthermore, there are other verses in the Church Epistles that mention prophets, such as 1 Corinthians 12:28 and Titus 1:12. Acts confirms what the Church Epistles teach, and shows that prophets were active and important in the Church (Acts 11:27, 13:1, 15:32, 21:10). Surely the Lord would not have specifically placed men and women in the Church with the gift ministry of a prophet if they did not perform a distinctly different role than other Christians who were operating the manifestation of prophecy.

In contrast to the manifestation of prophecy every Christian can operate, the gift ministry of a prophet is a specific calling of the Lord on a person's life. Thus the call to be a prophet is a job assignment, given to someone whether he wants it or not. The Old Testament scriptures make this very clear. Isaiah knew he was called from birth: "…Before I was born the LORD [Yahweh] called me; from my birth he has made mention of my name" (Isa. 49:1b). Amos describes the call of God upon his life: "…I was neither a prophet nor a prophet's son, but I was a shepherd, and I also took care of sycamore-fig trees. But the LORD [Yahweh] took me from tending the flock and said to me, 'Go, prophesy to my people Israel'" (Amos 7:14 and 15).

In regard to prophets in the Church, the book of Acts confirms what Ephesians and Corinthians state doctrinally, that the Lord selects and specifically calls some men and women to be prophets. Prophets were important in the establishment of the church at Antioch, the first church recorded that was composed of both Jews and Gentiles (Acts 11:27). It was the prophet Agabus who foretold that there would be a severe famine in the Roman world during the reign of Claudius Caesar (Acts 11:28; this famine is documented in secular Roman history). Prophets were vital in getting the revelation from the Lord to set apart Paul and Barnabas and send them on their first missionary journey (Acts 13:1-4). The prophets Judas and Silas are specifically mentioned as exhorting and confirming the disciples in Antioch (Acts 15:32-KJV). It was Agabus the prophet who so graphically portrayed what would happen to Paul in Jerusalem (Acts 21:10 and 11). In fact, the only foretelling in Acts is given either by prophets or by the apostles Peter and Paul.[1]

The book of Acts and the Church Epistles show clearly that the Lord still works through called prophets. They are not "just another believer because every Christian can prophesy," as some have stated. Evangelists still exist in the Church even though every Christian can share his faith, there are still pastors even though every Christian can help people

---

1. There are occasions when apostles, because of the position God has given them in the governance of the Church, are given words of prophecy that ordinarily would come to the Church through prophets. We see this in the book of Acts.

who are hurting, and there are still prophets in the Church even though every Christian can manifest prophecy. Prophets are charged with being spokesmen for God just as they were in the Old Testament, and today they speak also for the Lord Jesus Christ. Once we understand that the ministry of a prophet is the Lord's doing, and that they are very important to the health and wellbeing of the Church, we should be very interested in recognizing who they are and what we can do to help them in their job of being spokesmen so we can have the word of the Lord among us in a more powerful way.

Now that we know the difference between the manifestation of prophecy and the ministry of a prophet, we need to understand how that difference plays out in the Church. All prophecy, whether from a Christian operating the manifestation of prophecy, or from a called prophet, will be **as the Spirit gives utterance** (Acts 2:4-KJV). All true words of prophecy come from God or the Lord Jesus Christ, never from the speaker's mind. In the case of the manifestation of prophecy, the Lord limits himself to giving words of "…strengthening, encouragement, and comfort" (1 Cor. 14:3).[2] However, that is not the case with the ministry of a prophet. Called prophets speak the message the Lord gives them, whatever it may be. Both the manifestation of prophecy and the ministry of a prophet are used by the Lord in the Church today (Eph. 4:11).

To understand how prophets operate in the Church, we must understand how they functioned in the Old Testament. The various Greek and Hebrew words that are translated "prophet" or "seer" help a lot in understanding both what a prophet is and how God works with them. By far the most common word translated "prophet" in the Old Testament is *nabiy*, which means "spokesman." First and foremost, the prophet is a "spokesman" for God. The prophet must be able to hear the voice of God and bring God's words to the world.

Soon after Adam and Eve were driven from the Garden, God stopped

---

2. This is the usual case as is stated in the Word. Of course, the Lord can work through people who are not called prophets if he so desires, but that would be the exception, not the rule.

talking openly to people and chose specific individuals through whom He would communicate to mankind. Thus, by the first time the word "prophet" is used in the Bible, which was in the days of Abraham (Gen. 20:7, about 2,000 years after Adam), what a prophet did was no mystery to people. When God spoke in a dream to Abimelech king of Gerar and identified Abraham as a prophet, Abimelech did not say, "Hey God, what is a 'prophet'?" He knew exactly what a prophet was—a person who could hear the voice of God and communicate it to others.

The Greek word translated "prophet," *prophetes*, also shows that prophets are God's (or "the god's") chosen spokesmen. The noun *prophetes* is found in Greek writings as early as the 600's B.C., and it is related to the verb meaning to publicly speak forth or make known. The oldest occurrence we have today relates to a prophetic utterance at the oracle of Zeus at Dodona. Thus, ancient Greek language and culture confirms what the Hebrew language communicates: that even ancient pagan people realized that the words of the gods needed to be spoken forth and made known, and furthermore that the gods chose certain people through whom they spoke.[3] The New Testament use of *prophetes*, or prophet, is in line with that and means "One who, moved by the Spirit of God and hence his...spokesman, solemnly declares to men what he has received..."[4]

Because the prophet speaks the message that God gives him to speak, it can be as varied as God wants it to be. This is an important point, because often people try to "put God in a box" and decide what a prophetic message would look like, as if we could tell God what to say. It is beyond the scope of this appendix to categorize every type of message that prophets bring forth, but a short list will show some of the variation

---

3. Many people who have the gift ministry of a prophet do not serve the true God, but turn to the flesh or the demonic. Even then they are especially spiritually sensitive and are sometimes recognized as such. Thus they occasionally use their gifting for the Devil's purposes, and become psychics, mediums, oracles, "spiritual advisors," etc. The spiritual sensitivity of these people is real, whether they work for God or the Devil.

4. Joseph H. Thayer, *Thayer's Greek-English Lexicon of the New Testament* (Hendrickson Publishers, Peabody, MA, reprinted 2000), *"prophetes,"* p. 553.

that occurs in the Bible. In some categories there are many examples, but a few will suffice.

Prophets:

- Tell what will happen in the future: 1 Samuel 10:1-6; Isaiah 52:13-53:12; Matthew 24:2; Acts 11:28, 21:11
- Speak of past events: Judges 6:7-10; 2 Samuel 12:7 and 8; Ezekiel 20:1-31; John 4:18.
- Strengthen ("edification" KJV): 2 Samuel 7:8-12; Haggai 2:1-5
- Exhort: 2 Chronicles 15:1-7; Isaiah 35:1-4; Haggai 1:3-12
- Comfort: 1 Samuel 9:20; 2 Chronicles 20:15-17; Jeremiah 45:1-5
- Bless: Genesis 48:20; Deuteronomy 33:1; Joshua 14:13
- Curse: Joshua 8:26, 9:22 and 23; 2 Kings 2:24; Jeremiah 48:10
- Call out kings and ministries: 1 Samuel 10:1, 16:13; 1 Kings 11:29-39, 19:15-19; 2 Kings 9:1-13
- Reprove (sometimes harshly): 2 Samuel 12:1-14; Isaiah 22:15-25; Jeremiah 36:30 and 31; Malachi 2:3; Matthew 16:23, 23:12-36
- Foretell death or disaster: 1 Samuel 2:27-36; 1 Kings 13:20-24, 22:17-37; Jeremiah 28:16, 29:21; Amos 7:14-17
- Direct: Judges 4:4-6; 2 Kings 4:1-7, 5:10, 6:8-10; Jeremiah 32:13-15
- Name (showing God's opinion): 2 Samuel 12:25; Jeremiah 20:3
- Reveal character and what is in a person's heart: Isaiah 9:9 and 17, 29:13, 48:4; Jeremiah 2:21, 5:23; Ezekiel 14:2-4; John 1:47
- Interpret enigmas: Daniel 5:5-29
- Reveal what is going on from a spiritual perspective: 1 Chronicles 5:20; Jeremiah 1:16; Ezekiel 5:11; Daniel 9:11; John 8:42-47

Furthermore, prophets:

- Can have messages for individuals: 1 Samuel 10:1-6, for groups: 2 Kings 3:12-19, or for entire nations: Amos 1:11-2:16
- Have given prophecies to people about a third party: 1 Kings 14:7; 2 Kings 1:3
- May deliver the message themselves, or through others: 2 Kings 5:10, 9:1
- May interpret other people's dreams: Genesis 40:8-22, 41:15-28; Daniel 2:1-45, 4:4-37 (or their own as in Daniel 7)
- Might not get a revelation about a situation immediately: Jeremiah 28:5-17 (especially verse 11), 42:7
- May be called upon by God to act out their prophetic message: Jeremiah 19:1-13, 27:2, 43:8-13; Ezekiel 4:1-3, 9-17, 5:1-4, 12:1-11; Hosea 1:2; Acts 21:11
- May get revelation they do not understand: Numbers 12:6-8; Daniel 12:8; Zechariah 1:8 and 9

The point of the above list is to show clearly that prophets speak what they hear from God or the Lord Jesus, and that can be as varied as God wants it to be. Of course, because the prophet is a prophet of God, He will not contradict what He has said in His written Word. This brings up the fact that some people assert that God would not give a harsh word of reproof today because we live in the Age of Grace, but that assertion misses the point. The "grace" in the Age of Grace concerns what God has done for people through His Son: things like saved by grace and not by works, having permanent salvation, and being sealed with holy spirit. The "grace" in the Age of Grace certainly does not mean that we have the "grace" to live profligate lives without the Lord being upset and speaking frankly to us about it.

There are verses that apply to the Church that show God will still reprove and correct His people. The principle still stands: "...From everyone who has been given much, much will be demanded..." (Luke 12:48b). Sin is still sin, and just as God was so upset by the sin and hardheartedness of his "chosen people" in the Old Testament that He occasionally reproved them harshly, He can get just as upset at His chosen children today. Actually, since we have more today, we could reasonably expect Him to get more upset. Because Scripture says, "For it is time for judgment to begin with the family of God…" (1 Pet. 4:17a), God has some harsh punishment for those who turn from Him and have "…insulted the Spirit of grace" (Heb. 10:29, cp. 1 Thess. 4:6). Joseph Dillow writes:

> "Once a man is born again in Christ, he is now in God's family, and as any human father would, our divine Father takes a more personal interest in the moral behavior of those who belong to Him than to those outside the household of faith."[5]

Another Hebrew word translated "prophet" shows that prophets speak what they hear from God (or today from the Lord Jesus), and they do not speak on their own. The Hebrew word *nataph*, sometimes translated "prophet," means to drop, drip, or distill. Its uses include rain distilling and dripping from the sky, words that "drop" out of someone's mouth, and wine dripping from the mountains in Paradise. Although prophets are called upon to "drop" words where and when God demands, the more obvious thing we learn from *nataph* is that God drops His words upon the prophet. It means, as Strong's Concordance says, "to speak by inspiration." This means that the message the prophet brings is not his own message, but the Lord's words, and furthermore it implies that many times the prophet may not know much of the message when he starts prophesying, but that the words "drop" upon him, i.e., he speaks them as he gets them from God.

Two more Hebrew words that help us understand how God works in prophets are both translated "seer." One is *raah*, which means, "to see" (as with the eye), and the other is *chozeh*, which means "one who has a vision" (from *chazon*, "vision"). By virtue of the gift of holy spirit upon them and the revelation they received from God, prophets "saw" things that other people could not see. This was very apparent to the people around them, who used the term "seer" for the practical reason that they could see what

5. Joseph C. Dillow, *The Reign of the Servant Kings* (Schoettle Publishing Company, Hayesville, NC, 1993), p. 341.

was unseen by others. As God gave him revelation, a prophet could "see" into the future (Dan. 2:29-45), or into someone's heart (Ezek. 14:3).

The word "seer" has another overtone as well. Although there are well documented times when God spoke audibly to prophets, it seems the more common means of communication He used was visual revelation, even if the vision were in a dream. Although it would be ideal if every dream and vision were crystal clear and self-explanatory, that is not the case. The method and content of the visions and dreams of God are His business, and He has purposely chosen to be unclear in some of His communication. Although the tendency of most people is to blame the prophet for any unclear dream or revelation (and it is true that sin can cloud clear revelations from the Lord), this blame is often misplaced. God can be perfectly clear when He wants to be, as many Old and New Testament records attest.

Many biblical records show that God is purposely unclear. Numbers 12:6-8 indicates that God spoke to prophets in riddles, while to Moses He spoke "face to face," i.e., clearly. Proverbs 25:2 says it is the glory of God to conceal things. Furthermore, the Bible has records of prophets receiving visions and revelations they did not understand. For example, Daniel did not understand the meaning of what he heard (Dan. 12:8), Zechariah was shown a vision that he did not understand (Zech. 1:8 and 9), and Peter did not grasp what the Lord was communicating by the sheet full of unclean animals, argued with the Lord about it, and ended up "…wondering about the meaning of the vision…" (Acts 10:17).

There seem to be two primary reasons why God is sometimes purposely unclear. One is to drive people into deeper and more intimate communication with Him. Remember, the reason anyone gets any revelation in the first place is that God loves us, wants to help and bless us, and wants a relationship with us. But He does not want to be thought of as only "the Provider" from whom we can get things and then go our own way. He wants us to have a relationship with Him. How does a mother feel when she works hard to make a nice dinner and then kids come in and scarf it down in two minutes so they can watch a television show and leave without even saying "Thank you"? She wanted more from her children than just to be thought of as "the cook" or "the provider." So it is with God. There is more to life than just providing for others. God wants our love and to have a relationship with us. When there is unclear revelation, we are driven deeper and deeper into His heart as we seek understanding. We want to know what He meant, and that means we need to go to Him for the understanding.

The second reason that God (or the Lord) is sometimes unclear when He gives a revelation or a vision is that it causes people to work together. God is very desirous that His people work together, so He often gives out the "revelation pie" in pieces, so people have to get together to see the whole pie. We see this in the prophetic books in the Bible. There are many biblical topics that can be understood only by learning about them from several different books. God gave one revelation to the prophet Jeremiah, another to Ezekiel, another to Daniel, etc, and only when they are taken together do we get the whole picture. This is still true today, God giving a message through one prophet that is confirmed and developed by another prophet. Similarly, one prophet often has insights about the prophetic revelation that another prophet received, which sheds light on the original revelation.

Another reason for God to promote community and communication among the prophets is the need for prophets to mature in their calling. Being around other prophets helps a younger or less mature prophet grow and understand the revelation he or she is receiving. As early as the time of Samuel, prophets were companying together (1 Sam. 10:5), and Samuel is sometimes credited with starting what is called, "the school of the prophets."[6]

Realizing prophets need to grow and mature in their walk with God helps us understand better how to relate to them, and also why the Lord says prophets are to "weigh carefully" each other's words (1 Cor. 14:29). It is important to understand that even mature prophets can be wrong, or appear wrong, in what they say. For that reason, accountability to other prophets

---

6. For more on the school of the prophets, see "Chapter Six," Number 17, "Team prophecy can be a blessing."

and to the Body of Christ is very important. The prophetic minister must have the courage to deliver God's message but also recognize that he or she does not stand alone. The goal of the prophet is not to tear down but to recover and build up. Building up the Body of Christ is a challenging goal that can be accomplished only by cooperation with, and accountability to, other believers in the Body of Christ.

Prophets, while calling others to account, must also be accountable. In that light, every prophet must realize that he or she is engaged in a spiritual battle, and the primary weapon of that warfare is the Word of God. The Lord's prophets must strive to prophesy and interpret dreams and visions in accordance with the written Word of God, understanding that now we see through a glass darkly. Because people can still be influenced by their flesh and give inaccurate prophecies, all Christians are told to "weigh carefully" the prophetic words of others.[7]

Because of their prominent position in the Body of Christ, and because it is easy to be influenced by the flesh, it is of utmost importance that prophets maintain holy and obedient lifestyles. God considers it "horrible" when prophets live sinful lives (Jer. 23:14). A prophet is to anchor his life in prayer, and focus on the Hope even when the task at hand seems hopeless. This requires determination and discipline. Another quality the prophet must have is the courage to deliver God's message no matter what the content. Because the fallen nature of man is constantly bringing him downward, a good portion of a prophet's work comes in the form of reproof and correction. This can easily be seen by reading the prophetic books and noting what the prophets said. Things are no different now in the Administration of Grace than they were in the Old Testament. The sin nature of man exerts a strong influence, which is why there is so much reproof and correction even in the Church Epistles.

Speaking words of reproof and correction is rarely a blessing. The

---

7. It is important to correctly understand 1 Corinthians 14:29, which reads: "Two or three prophets should speak, and the others should weigh carefully what is said." Although "others" refers to prophets, it also includes the rest of the congregation, each of whom has holy spirit and each of whom should be interested in the prophetic word being accurate.

heavy nature of many prophetic utterances is why revelation from God was often called a "burden." For example:

- "The burden of the word of the LORD to Israel by Malachi" (Mal. 1:1-KJV).
- "The burden of Nineveh. The book of the vision of Nahum the Elkoshite" (Nah. 1:1-KJV).
- "The burden which Habakkuk the prophet did see" (Hab. 1:1-KJV).
- "The burden of the word of the LORD ..." (Zech. 9:1-KJV). The NIV and many other more modern versions say "oracle" or some other similar translation, but "burden" is the proper translation.[8]

The prophet must also develop the wisdom to deliver his message the way the Lord would have it delivered. This means that he must endeavor to have the heart of the Lord for people. Because prophetic utterances can have a huge impact on the one receiving the message, it is very important that the prophet deliver the message with the same heart as the Lord would if he were here personally. That does not mean that the message will always be gentle ("...Get behind me, Satan!...") was hardly gentle), but it does mean that it will be delivered the way the Lord would have it delivered.

It is a very difficult task to distill to doctrine the communication that a prophet receives by revelation and how it should (or perhaps should not) be communicated to others. The mature prophet knows that sometimes the Lord communicates to him in a manner that is meaningful only to him, and a literal recitation of it would only be misunderstood by a listener. In such cases, the prophet gives the Lord's message, and not the literal vision or revelation he received, so that the listener gets the message that the Lord meant for him.

The Lord often uses harsh words or striking images to create impact, perhaps like a figure of speech makes an impact in literature. Mature

---

8. R. Harris, G. Archer, B. Waltke, *Theological Wordbook of the Old Testament* (Moody Press, Chicago, 1980), Vol. 1, pp. 1421 and 1422.

prophets do not assume that stark imagery is literally true, but nor do they discount that it may be. The prophet's task is to discern the truth being conveyed, and then to communicate that truth as accurately and lovingly as possible. This communication may take a number of forms and will not always be accepted or understood. A wise prophet will seek the Lord for wisdom concerning the details, timing and wording for each situation. He or she may also seek counsel of trusted advisors or more seasoned prophets. This however, provides no guarantee that the message or the prophet will not be criticized or disregarded.

Just as prophets get lauded and praised when their prophecies are a blessing, they are derided and persecuted when their prophecies are unexpected or unwanted. Prophets must accept this in order to forestall temptations of disobedience, self pity, envy, bitterness, and hardheartedness, and to be able to see and hear clearly the revelation that the Lord wants communicated.

Each prophet must develop his own relationship with the Lord Jesus so that the Lord can communicate to him in a way that he understands, even if others do not. There will be times when it would be detrimental for the prophet to repeat exactly what the Lord gives to him because the images would be misunderstood. Each prophet must learn from experience how to correctly understand the messages and images he receives from the Lord, and then prophesy to others in a way that is helpful and appropriate.

One of the great services that the prophets of old performed was to help people who needed to know what to do about specific situations. 1 Samuel 9:9 shows that people regularly went to prophets to get information they needed.

1 Samuel 9:9
(Formerly in Israel, if a man went to inquire of God, he would say, "Come, let us go to the seer," because the prophet of today used to be called a seer.)

Knowing the right thing to do in a specific situation has always been a challenge, and the Adversary has worked hard to deceive God's people by providing demonic sources of spiritual information. Many people today call a psychic hotline or go to a medium, tarot card reader, or "spiritual advisor" when they need advice, and many others read the daily horoscope to find out what to do or not do on a given day. That prophecy has been weak and even nonexistent in the Church has added to the problem. Although some people who look to demonic sources of information are Christians, they may not know that what they are doing is a sin in the eyes of God, and they usually do not have a clue that they can tap into their gift of holy spirit to get a message of knowledge and a message of wisdom, or go to a prophet in the Church for help and direction.

There has always been spiritual advice available, both good and bad. That is why the Bible mentions and forbids the practice of divination, consulting mediums, astrology, etc. (cp. Deut. 18:9-13). Kings have always surrounded themselves with men who claimed to have supernatural knowledge. Pharaoh of Egypt is one example (Gen. 41:8) and Nebuchadnezzar is another (Dan. 2:1-3). Even though the majority of the sources of spiritual advice most people today know about are demonic, there is also spiritual advice available from the true God.

The Bible has many examples of people going to a prophet to seek the will of God, and He got very upset if they went to other spiritual sources. Divination, mediums, astrology, etc., were all forbidden. God wanted the people to seek Him, and that usually meant through the prophets or priests. In the Old Testament, people knew that if the Lord had any guidance for them, they could get it by going to a prophet. Examples of people seeking prophecy for specific reasons include:

1 Samuel 9:6	Saul went to Samuel to find his lost animals.
1 Samuel 9:9	The people of Israel went to the prophet to inquire of God.
1 Samuel 22:15	David had sought the will of God from Ahimelech the priest.
1 Samuel 23:1-12	David four times sought God's will through Abiathar the priest.

1 Samuel 28:6	Saul sought information from prophets, but there was no revelation.
1 Kings 14:1-3	Jeroboam sent to Ahijah the prophet to find out about his child.
1 Kings 22:4-28	Jehoshaphat sought a prophet to find out if he should go to war.
2 Kings 3:11	Jehoshaphat sought the will of God from Elisha.
2 Kings 4:1-7	The widow sought the help of God from Elisha.
2 Kings 4:21-37	The Shunammite woman sought the help of Elijah for her dead son.
2 Kings 5:3	The maid wanted Naaman to visit the prophet in Samaria.
2 Kings 8:7 and 8	Hazael sent to Elisha to see if he would recover from his sickness.
2 Kings 19:1-7	Hezekiah sent to Isaiah to find out about the Assyrian attack.
2 Kings 22:11-20	Josiah sent to Huldah the prophetess to find out what to do.
Jeremiah 21:1-14	Zedekiah sent to Jeremiah to know if Jerusalem would be delivered.
Jeremiah 37:17	Zedekiah sent to Jeremiah to see if there was a word from the LORD.
Jeremiah 38:14-26	Zedekiah sent for Jeremiah to ask him questions.

There is a spiritual war going on between God and the Devil, and each person must choose the source from which he will get his information. It is sad that the prophetic word in the Church has been so weak, or even nonexistent, that people are flocking to psychic hotlines, tarot cards, astrology, and mediums to get the information they want. As the ministry of the prophet is restored in the Church, Christians will be able to seek information from the Lord's prophets rather than demonic sources. Of course, many of the questions that people ask on psychic hotlines are not the kind of questions the Lord will give an answer to, but the prophets could tell that directly to the one asking.

A study of the biblical examples of people seeking prophecy reveals that the prophet does not always have to rely solely on revelation for information. For example, in the record of the widow who asked Elisha for help (2 Kings 4 in the list above), he got the details of the situation from the widow herself before he got the word from the LORD. If you are called as a prophet, you should desire to restore the position of the prophet in the Church and be blessed at the opportunity to seek the Lord for people. Then if you get a word, wonderful. If not, the person is no worse off than when he came to you. Similarly, we in the Church should be encouraging the prophets and looking to them to help us get direction from the Lord in our lives.

Some people say: "Well, the only reason people in the Old Testament had to go to prophets was because they did not have holy spirit and could not go to God for themselves." That thinking is not correct. While it is true that most people did not have holy spirit upon them, some who did still sought information from prophets. David and other kings had prophets in their courts, and a study of David's life shows that he regularly asked prophets for information even though he had holy spirit. Sometimes, when a person is in a really difficult situation, it is difficult to calm down enough to hear the voice of the Lord. It is usually much easier for someone who is not as close to the situation to hear from the Lord.

The ministry of the prophet is not in evidence in the Church as it should be, nor, I believe, as the Lord wants it to be. Where are the prophets who warn us of destructive weather or economic disaster? Where are the prophets who call out the ministries in our churches? Where are the prophets who advise our army and our government, and indeed, give personal advice and direction so people will see that there is a God in heaven? In Amos 3:7, God said, "Surely the Sovereign LORD does nothing without revealing his plan to his servants the prophets." Yet, today, much happens without any prophetic input at all. Every Christian can hear from the Lord, and should push himself to do so. But we also need to pray and ask the Lord to continue to add prophets to the Church so that we can have more of his words and wisdom as it applies to specific situations.

We also should do more to encourage the prophets to hear the call of the Lord and develop themselves in their ministries. We need to support them as they grow in their walk, encouraging them to be pure and holy so the word they hear will be pure and not compromised by the flesh (this applies to all of us as Christians who want to hear from the Lord). Are we afraid that bold prophets would be dictators? Are we, as the Israelites of old, so entangled in the flesh that we do not want prophets who can see into our hearts and call us to account? Are our lives so full already that we do not want prophets directing us to do more than we are already doing? Are we so unwilling to listen and change that the Lord simply will not speak? We, God's Church and Christ's Body, must be willing to seek first the kingdom of God in order to have the ministries Christ has given work effectively in the Church.

"Lord Jesus, if it was God's heart in the Old Testament not to act without telling His prophets, that must be your heart today. Yet there are so many areas in which we are blind and deaf. Has our sin driven you away from us? Have our efforts to know you been half-hearted and self-serving? Help us to be deserving of your active participation in our lives. Help us to want to hear clearly from you. Lord Jesus, raise up and energize a company of prophets, men and women who will boldly and clearly bring your words to your Church. Amen."

APPENDIX B
False Prophets and False Prophecies

It is a common Christian teaching that if a prophecy is given but does not come to pass, the one who gave the prophecy is a false prophet and, at least in Old Testament times, would have been put to death. That teaching is in error. Given what we know about the conditional nature of prophecy (see chapter two), and also that prophecies usually require faith, prayer, and work on the part of the one who received it in order to be fulfilled, true prophets of God can speak by revelation and the prophecy not come to pass. Moses was not a false prophet even though Canaan was not completely conquered, Jonah was not a false prophet even though Nineveh was not destroyed, and Agabus was not a false prophet even though the Jews did not bind Paul and deliver him to the Romans (instead the Romans saved Paul from being beaten to death by the Jews; Acts 21:11, 30-33). In contrast, a false prophet is not one whose words do not come to pass, but rather one who gets information from a demonic source and/or leads people away from the true God. This fact is made clear in the following verses:

Deuteronomy 13:1-5

(1) If a prophet, or one who foretells by dreams, appears among you and announces to you a miraculous sign or wonder,

(2) and if the sign or wonder of which he has spoken takes place, and he says, "Let us follow other gods" (gods you have not known) "and let us worship them,"

(3) you must not listen to the words of that prophet or dreamer. The LORD your God is testing you to find out whether you love him with all your heart and with all your soul.

(4) It is the LORD your God you must follow, and him you must revere. Keep his commands and obey him; serve him and hold fast to him.

(5) That prophet or dreamer must be put to death, because he preached rebellion against the LORD your God, who brought you out of Egypt and redeemed you from the land of slavery; he has

tried to turn you from the way the LORD your God commanded you to follow. You must purge the evil from among you.

These verses make it plain that a false prophet is not just a prophet whose words do not come to pass. According to verse 2 above, the prophecy did come to pass, but the prophet in question was still considered a false prophet and put to death because he was trying to lead the people away from the true God. This shows that simply giving a prophecy that comes to pass does not make someone a true prophet of God.

It is important to realize that false prophets are not "false" because what they say is wrong. They are "false" because they do not represent the "true" God. Balaam was a prophet who stood against God, yet everything the Bible records him prophesying was true. The Devil knows the facts of a situation and is not shy about using his prophets to reveal it. The woman with the spirit of divination (Acts 16:16-KJV) spoke the truth about Paul and his companions, but she was a false prophet and spoke via a demon, ultimately turning people away from Paul and the truth he presented.

Deuteronomy 18 contains a significant section about prophecy.

Deuteronomy 18:20
But a prophet who presumes to speak in my name anything I have not commanded him to say, or a prophet who speaks in the name of other gods, **must be put to death**."

The NIV translation of verse 20 assumes too much. The translation, "must be put to death" is not what the Hebrew text says, but is an assumption about what it means. What the Hebrew text actually says is better translated in the KJV:

Deuteronomy 18:20 (KJV)
But the prophet, which shall presume to speak a word in my name, which I have not commanded him to speak, or that shall speak in the name of other gods, even **that prophet shall die**.

The words, "shall die" do not indicate the means of death. A study of the phrase reveals that sometimes it means, "shall be put to death," as the NIV translators assume it means, but it can also mean, "shall die" in a purely factual sense. There are many examples showing the two ways this phrase can be translated. For instance, Deuteronomy 17:12, 22:25 and 24:7 are uses of the phrase when it clearly means "execute" or "put to death," and 1 Samuel 2:34; 1 Kings 14:12 and Proverbs 15:10, 19:16 are uses of the phrase where it simply means to die.[1] Thus, the phrase itself is not conclusive, and a study of its context and the scope of Scripture is required to discover which of the two meanings it has in any given verse. Deuteronomy continues about prophecy:

Deuteronomy 18:21 and 22
(21) You may say to yourselves, "How can we know when a message has not been spoken by the LORD?"
(22) If what a prophet proclaims in the name of the LORD does not take place or come true, that is a message the LORD has not spoken. That prophet has spoken presumptuously. Do not be afraid of him.

Verse 22 contains an interesting piece of information that helps us understand exactly what is being said in this section of Scripture. If a prophet speaks something in the name of the LORD that does not come to pass, the people should simply "not be afraid of him." When we put verse 22 together with Deuteronomy 13:5 and 18:20, an interesting picture develops. If a prophet speaks to people with the intent of leading them away from God, he "must be put to death." On the other hand, if a prophet speaks in the name of the LORD and the prophecy does not come to pass, perhaps it is conditional. How would the people know? In any case, the people should not be afraid of him and, if he is a false prophet, he "shall die."

The Bible has examples of prophets who spoke prophecies that were

---

1. Because every human "shall die," the obvious meaning is that the false prophet shall die before his natural time. There is, however, the overtone of everlasting death, especially because false prophets will not be in the Resurrection of the Just.

not from God and who died. One of the most interesting is in the book of Jeremiah. Nebuchadnezzar's army had attacked Judah and taken people and material goods back to Babylon. Jeremiah had foretold that the Babylonian captivity would last 70 years (Jer. 25:11 and 12). However, another prophet, Hananiah, challenged Jeremiah and said that the captivity would be two years or less (Jer. 28:3). How were the people going to know the truth? What happened in this situation of "dueling prophets"?

Jeremiah 28:15-17

(15) Then the prophet Jeremiah said to Hananiah the prophet, "Listen, Hananiah! The LORD has not sent you, yet you have persuaded this nation to trust in lies.
(16) Therefore, this is what the LORD says: 'I am about to remove you from the face of the earth. This very year you are going to die, because you have preached rebellion against the LORD.'"
(17) In the seventh month of that same year, Hananiah the prophet died.

Hananiah turned out to be the false prophet, and he died before the two year time period ended. He died, fulfilling the words of Deuteronomy, but he was not executed by the people. Eli and Amaziah were priests, but it can reasonably be assumed from the culture and their position that they prophesied at least occasionally, and both of them also died of unnatural causes without being executed (1 Sam. 4:18; Amos 7:17). It is very important when considering this subject to realize **the Bible does not have even one example of a prophet being executed when his prophecies did not come to pass**. That, combined with the fact Deuteronomy does not require a prophet whose prophecy did not come to pass to be executed, is very strong evidence that just because a prophecy does not come to pass does not mean the prophet should be executed (Old Testament) or necessarily considered an ungodly person (as is often the case today).

The Bible does have examples of prophets who were put to death when they led the people to worship other gods. Elijah had the 450 prophets of Baal put to death, and Jehu had the prophets of Baal executed (1 Kings 18:40; 2 Kings 10:18-31).

Besides false prophets being executed for leading people from the true God, true prophets were sometimes executed or imprisoned because they challenged the political system of the time. John the Baptist is the most prominent example. He rightly challenged the sexual behavior of Herod Antipas, the king, telling him it was not lawful to have his brother's wife (Mark 6:18). John did not foretell the future, so he was not judged by whether or not what he said came to pass. He was imprisoned and eventually executed for telling the truth to a ruthless and powerful person who did not want to hear it.

Jeremiah foretold the destruction of Jerusalem, and when the people of Jerusalem heard his words, they said, "...This man should be sentenced to death because he has prophesied against this city [Jerusalem]..." (Jer. 26:11). The people did not care whether his words came to pass or not, which of course they did. They were going to put him to death for speaking against their sin and against the city of Jerusalem. In a similar vein, Micaiah was imprisoned when he spoke against the king of Israel long before it was known whether what he said was right or wrong (1 Kings 22:27). What Micaiah said also came to pass. Asa, king of Judah, threw Hanani the prophet in prison for reproving him (2 Chron. 16:7-10). Amaziah, king of Judah, threatened to kill a prophet if he did not stop his prophetic reproof (2 Chron. 25:15 and 16), and there were others, such as Jezebel (1 Kings 18:13), who killed the prophets of God for political or religious reasons of their own.

From the evidence in Scripture, it is improper to conclude that if a prophecy does not come to pass, the prophet is a false prophet. True prophets can speak prophecies that do not come to pass for a number of reasons: because of the conditional nature of prophecy; because the people who receive the prophecy do not do the work required for it to be fulfilled; or because the nature of personal prophecy focuses more on the "take home message" than specific details, so sometimes details do not seem to be correct (as in the prophecy of Agabus).

In contrast, Scripture reveals that false prophets can give prophecies (and do signs and wonders) that are accurate and do come to pass.

However, false prophets will ultimately lead people away from God and His written Word whether what they say comes to pass or not. Psychics and mediums do this consistently. They are "spiritual" people, but they are not spiritual in the godly sense of the word. They are in contact with demons, but usually they, and the people they advise, do not know it. This is just one more reason why each Christian needs a good understanding of the Bible. When we know the truth set forth in the Bible, we know when we are being led away from it. If we do not know it, we can ignorantly be led into sin, and away from God.

The student of prophecy who understands the above information realizes the complexity of prophecy. Both false prophets and genuine prophets can speak prophecies that are factually correct and/or come to pass. Similarly, both false prophets and genuine prophets can speak prophecies that are not factually correct or do not come to pass. Therefore, looking at whether or not a prophecy comes to pass is not the ultimate test of a true prophet. It may be an indicator, especially over time, but it is not conclusive.

By having an understanding of how prophecy works, we will not fall into the trap of castigating or ostracizing a true prophet who had a prophecy not come to pass, or accepting into our Christian ranks a false prophet whose words have come true.

APPENDIX C
Dreams

The subject of dreams is an important one because God said He would speak to people through them (Joel 2:28; Acts 2:17). Of course, not all dreams are from God. The three sources of dreams are God (or the Lord Jesus), one's mind, and demons. We will examine each of these.

Dreams can come from one's mind, especially when the person is under a lot of stress. Ecclesiastes makes it clear when people are stressed or anxious, they tend to dream: "As a dream comes when there are many cares…" (Eccles. 5:3a). Isaiah 29:8 gives the example of a man who is stressed because he is hungry dreaming he is eating, and a man who is stressed because he is thirsty dreaming that he is drinking. God did not give those dreams by revelation; they arose out of the anxiety and stress of life.[1]

Another source of dreams is demons. Jeremiah 23:25 and 32; and Zechariah 10:2 are examples. Since there are several sources for dreams, it is very important to be sure that any dream you think is from God actually is from Him. God cautions against a person having dream after dream and trying to run his life by them.

Ecclesiastes 5:7
Much dreaming and many words are meaningless. Therefore stand in awe of God.

Ecclesiastes 5:3a states that some dreams come when there are many cares, and verse 7 cautions about trying to assign meanings to those many

---

[1]. It is important to differentiate between dreams given by revelation and dreams that are from the person's mind but are the result of the Lord working in his life. For example, if a person is praying to know what to do, and working to break out of comfort-zone living, he might have a dream that really helps him get things in focus. If the dream came by revelation, then it was directly from the Lord. But it could also be the result of the Lord working in his life and things "coming together for him" in his mind without the dream being direct revelation.

dreams. Instead, we are to "…stand in awe of God" by obeying His written Word, using our God-given knowledge and wisdom, and obeying the clear revelation we receive.

God (or the Lord Jesus), is the third source of dreams. If a dream is from God, then it is revelation and, like all revelation, will be either a message of knowledge or a message of wisdom. A revelation dream is not prophecy. If you believe the information in the dream was the Lord speaking to you about someone, and you communicate the word of the Lord to that person, the revelation you received becomes prophecy as you communicate it. As with any revelation, it is important to communicate it accurately.

Jeremiah 23:28a
"Let the prophet who has a dream tell his dream, but let the one who has my word speak it faithfully…

Entire books have been written on the subject of dreams, and this is not the place for an exhaustive study. Nevertheless, one thing is clear: much of what is in dreams is symbolic, and it requires prayer and seeking the Lord to understand them accurately. Having other prophets help interpret a particular dream may be necessary. In Genesis 40, Pharaoh's baker and cupbearer both dreamed, and they knew their dreams were from God, but they did not understand them. The same thing happened with Pharaoh in Genesis 41. In those cases, Joseph helped interpret the revelation they had received. In Judges 7:13 and 14, one man had a revelation dream but did not understand it, and another man helped with the interpretation. In Numbers 12:6-8, God contrasts the way He speaks to most prophets (in dreams, visions, and riddles), with the fact that He spoke with Moses "face to face."

Daniel 2 has the example of Nebuchadnezzar receiving revelation in a dream but not understanding what it meant, and having to seek help to get the interpretation. Unfortunately, some versions such as the KJV make it seem as if Nebuchadnezzar had forgotten his dream. He had not forgotten it at all, and other versions such as the NIV are much clearer in their translation. Daniel 4 is another example of Nebuchadnezzar having a dream that was revelation but needing help with the interpretation. Daniel was especially adept at helping people understand their dreams, and gained a reputation for that (Dan. 5:12).

We have seen in the body of this book that people can go to prophets and ask them to seek the Lord for information. Sometimes people have encouraged prophets who tend to receive revelation by dreams to dream for them. This occurred even in biblical times:

Jeremiah 29:8
Yes, this is what the LORD Almighty, the God of Israel, says: "Do not let the prophets and diviners among you deceive you. Do not listen to the dreams you encourage them to have."

Jeremiah was specifically referring to false prophets and dreamers who were being encouraged by the people. However, there is a general principle in this verse: if you want information from a prophet, the wisest path is to simply ask the prophet to "seek the Lord." Considering that dreams can be very symbolic and require further understanding and interpretation, to go to a prophet and ask specifically that he or she get a dream from the Lord for guidance is not prudent. Be thankful for an answer from the Lord, and do not try to dictate to him how he should answer.

Studying the dreams in the Bible that were from the true God reveals that a large percentage of them concern the one who did the dreaming. This is an important point, and it is wise to be cautious about heeding the dream of someone who considers himself a prophet but whose every dream is about other people. The way to evaluate a prophecy that originates in a dream is similar to the way to evaluate any prophecy. Who is the source? Does it line up with the written Word? Do you get an inner witness it is true? What do other prophets and seasoned believers say about it? Remember, dreams are only one way the Lord speaks, and they do not deserve "blind obedience." On the other hand, the Lord can speak very powerfully in dreams, and we need to be open to hearing his voice through them.

APPENDIX D
Revelation: What It Is and How It Is Received

What is Revelation?

The word "revelation" comes from the word "reveal." Revelation is "something that is revealed." Biblically, the word "revelation" refers to something revealed by a spiritual source, which may be God, the Lord Jesus Christ, the Devil, or demons. The "book of Revelation" is so called because its contents were revealed by God to Jesus, who revealed it to an angel, who revealed it to the Apostle John (Rev. 1:1). In its secular usage, "revelation" can refer to something that has a profound impact on a person or when someone learned something that helped him understand some aspect of life. For example, someone might say, "It was a revelation to me to learn that my headaches could be cured by getting more sleep." However, that is not the way "revelation" is used in its biblical context.

A. Revelation is not:

1. What someone learns from reading the Bible. When the Bible was originally given, it was revelation to that individual who then wrote it down. When a person reads it, he learns, but that type of learning is not revelation. It is available, however, for God to give someone revelation about what the Bible says so he can understand it clearly.

2. What someone feels very strongly about. When a person feels very strongly about something, there is a danger that some of those strong opinions will "leak over" into what he says comes from God. This is as true for doctrine as it is for personal feelings and opinions.

3. What someone knows from his five senses (seeing, hearing, smelling, tasting, and touching). What a person observes through his senses may be accurate, but something is not "revelation" unless it comes from a spiritual source.

B. Revelation is:

Information that is revealed to someone by a spiritual source. That source can be either good (God or Jesus), or it can be evil (the Devil or demons).

God's "Categories" of Revelation

God places revelation into two categories. These categories are:

> 1. A Message of Knowledge
>
> 2. A Message of Wisdom

These categories of revelation can be found in 1 Corinthians.

1 Corinthians 12:8

To one there is given through the Spirit the message of wisdom, to another the message of knowledge by means of the same Spirit,

All revelation will fall into one of these categories because revelation is either knowledge or wisdom. "Wisdom" has many aspects, and in today's language can have several definitions. However, as it is used in a biblical context, "wisdom" is the proper application of knowledge.[1] The first definition of "wisdom" in the first edition of *Webster's Dictionary* (published in 1828) captures its meaning when it comes to "a message of wisdom": "the right use or exercise of knowledge."[2]

The categories of revelation, i.e., a message of knowledge and a message of wisdom, are also the names of two manifestations of holy spirit. However, the revelation itself, the information, does not have to

---

1. For a further explanation of this, and why discerning of spirits is not a category of revelation, see our book, Chapter 8, "Walking in Power: The Manifestations of Holy Spirit," *op. cit., The Gift of Holy Spirit: The Power to be Like Christ.*
2. Noah Webster, *American Dictionary of the English Language* (Foundation for American Christian Education, San Francisco, CA, reprinted 1967) "wisdom," (book pages not numbered).

come via a manifestation, it could come via phenomenon.

We say that revelation is a "message" of knowledge or wisdom because the Greek word *logos* in 1 Corinthians 12:8 means "word," not as a "vocabulary word," but as an intelligent communication. The first definition of *logos* in *Thayer's Greek Lexicon* is "a word, yet not in the grammatical sense (equivalent to vocabulum, the mere name of an object), but language...a word which, uttered by the living voice, embodies a conception or idea."[3] The NIV uses "message," and other versions, such as the RSV, NRSV, and NJB, use "utterance," which would be fine as long as it is understood that it is the Lord who "utters" the message to the person and not that the person speaks a message of wisdom to someone else. God often gives revelation by sight, or a feeling, etc., and so for the new Christian, saying that revelation is a "word" might make it seem that revelation from God is supposed to be something that can be heard, which is not the case.

A brief definition of revelation is:

1. **A Message of Knowledge** is God or the Lord Jesus Christ providing to you information, insight, and understanding about something.

2. **A Message of Wisdom** is God or the Lord Jesus Christ providing to you direction, or how to apply the knowledge you have about something.

When God gives a revelation message to someone, that one message may contain both of the above categories. For example, when God gives a message of knowledge (i.e., gives a person information), He will often give with it a message of wisdom so the person knows what to do with the information he received. If there is no message of wisdom, it usually means what to do is clear from either the Word of God or from natural wisdom based on the physical universe, the five senses world. When a person receives a message for another by revelation (which is prophecy

---

3. Thayer, *op. cit., Thayer's Greek-English Lexicon*, p 380.

when spoken), and because revelation is either a message of knowledge or a message of wisdom, the prophecy will also be one or more of those—a message of knowledge or a message of wisdom.

How Revelation Comes to Individuals

Revelation, information from the spiritual world, is given to people in many different ways.

1. Direct communication. For example, God, Jesus, an angel, the Devil, or a demon, can appear to, or speak directly with, an individual.

- God (Gen. 18:1-15; Exod. 24:9-11; 1 Sam. 3:10; Isa. 6:1-13).[4]
- Jesus (Acts 7:55, 9:4-6, 10-16, 22:17-21; Gal. 1:12).
- An angel (Gen. 21:17; Judg. 6:11-22; Luke 1:11-20, 28-37; Acts 10:3-7).
- The Devil (Gen. 3:1-5; Matt. 4:3-11).
- A demon (1 Sam. 28:13-19).[5]

2. Communication from God or Jesus via holy spirit. God or the Lord Jesus communicates with the person via holy spirit, which indwells and fills him (Num. 11:16, 17 and 25; Joel 2:28; Luke 1:67; Acts 2:4; 1 Cor. 12:8).

3. Communication from a demon inhabiting the person. A demon inhabiting a person's mind (which some people refer to as "possession") gives him information. People hear voices, see images, or just "get ideas" (Num. 5:14-KJV; Jer. 2:8, 23:13; Hosea 4:12; Zech. 10:2).

4. Communication from others who have received revelation. Genuine prophets and indeed, in the Administration of Grace,

---

4. For a more thorough explanation of God appearing to people, and more examples, see our book, Appendix A, note on Genesis 18:1, *op. cit., One God & One Lord*, p. 439.

5. The "Samuel" that appeared to Saul was a demon impersonating Samuel. For more information, see our book *Is There Death After Life?* by Mark Graeser, John Lynn, John Schoenheit (Christian Educational Services, Indianapolis, IN, 5th edition, 2004), pp. 84 and 85.

any believer, can receive revelation and communicate it to others (Acts 9:10-16, 21:10 and 11). False prophets hear from the demonic side of the spiritual world and communicate that revelation to people. Mediums (those who directly consult the spirit world) and necromancers (people who "communicate with the dead") are specific types of such false prophets (Deut. 18:11).[6]

5. Communication via something in the physical world. Things that occur in the physical realm can sometimes have a spiritual source and communicate a message.[7] If a physical event had a spiritual cause, that cause can be either godly or demonic. However, it is sometimes difficult or even impossible to tell from the five senses whether the event had a godly source, a demonic source, or happened due to simple natural laws and only by coincidence ("chance") seemed to communicate something.

The difficulty of determining the source of something in the physical world can be seen in an example from history, as recorded in Ezekiel. Nebuchadnezzar cast lots with arrows, consulted idols, and looked at animal livers to try to discern what he should do (Ezek. 21:21). If the arrows fell and pointed toward Jerusalem, why? What was the cause or source? Was it God directing him to attack the disobedient Judeans, demons wanting to destroy God's people, or simply coincidence due to the fact that the arrows had to point somewhere when they fell?

Sometimes much prayer, wisdom, and counsel is needed to understand the actual cause of something in the physical world. Below are some examples from Scripture of the three possible sources when something occurs in the physical world.

---

6. Actually, dead people are not alive in any form, and cannot communicate at all. Demons impersonate dead people, which is why it is detestable to God to try to contact the dead (Deut. 18:12). Sadly, usually neither the necromancer nor the person seeking information knows they are communicating with a demon. *Ibid.,* for more information about death and the dead. You can read key sections/chapters online at www.TruthOrTradition.com TOPIC: Death or What Happens if You Die?

7. There are things in the physical realm that have a spiritual source but do not communicate a message. See "Miracle" and "Phenomenon" in the Glossary.

- **A godly cause:** Balaam's talking donkey (Num. 22:28-30); the dew on Gideon's fleece (Judg. 6:36-40); the sound in the balsam trees (2 Sam. 5:24); fire from the sky (1 Kings 18:24); the writing on the wall of Balthazar's palace (Dan. 5:5).

- **A demonic cause:** The magician's rods becoming serpents (Exod. 7:8-13)[8]; Simon's sorcery (Acts 8:9-12); and lying wonders (2 Thess. 2:9-KJV). "Divination" is getting information from a spiritual source via an object. Divination includes things such as reading tarot cards, crystal balls, palms, and tea leaves. Using a Ouija Board is divination, as is examining animal innards (Ezek. 21:21). All divination is an abomination to God because it is getting information from His archenemy, the Devil (Deut. 18:10-12). Astrology is another form of divination. God set the stars in place to tell us about Him and His plan, but astrology perverts that, turns it completely around, and says the stars tell us about ourselves.[9] Astrology is wrong in the eyes of God (Deut. 18:10[10]; Isa. 47:12-15).

- **A coincidence or "chance" occurrence.** Although some Christians teach that there is no such thing as "chance,"

---

8. The rod becoming a serpent was more than just a miracle. It was a "sign" with a "voice" that spoke of the true God. This point is clear in the Hebrew text and a few English versions. Exodus 4:8 (KJV): "And it shall come to pass, if they will not believe thee, neither hearken to the **voice** of the first sign, that they will believe the **voice** of the latter sign." Moses' rod spoke of the true God, the magician's rods answered back, but not with as powerful a message, seeing that Moses' rod ate the magician's rods. Nevertheless, Pharaoh would not hear the true God, or Moses and Aaron, His messengers.

9. For more information about how the stars reveal the true God and His plan of redemption, see E. W. Bullinger, *The Witness of the Stars* (Kregel Publications, Grand Rapids, MI, reprinted 1970), E. Raymond Capt, *The Glory of the Stars* (Artisan Sales, Thousand Oaks, CA, 1976), and Kenneth C. Fleming, *God's Voice in the Stars* (Loizeaux Brothers, Neptune, NJ, 1981).

10. The Hebrew word translated as "interprets omens" in Deuteronomy 18:10 includes the use of astrology. See, S. R. Driver, *The International Critical Commentary: Deuteronomy* (Edinburgh, T. & T. Clark, 1986), p. 225.

both the Bible and life testify otherwise. However, we must understand what "chance" is. Not everything that happens is caused by a spiritual source. God designed the physical universe to run by physical laws, and most of the time those laws operate without the intervention of a spiritual source. Although godly or demonic spirits can influence our physical world, much of the time they do not. For example, if your family is playing Monopoly, it is likely that neither God nor demons are influencing the role of the dice; instead, the laws of physics are at work. If a neighborhood kid hits a baseball through your window, it is unlikely "the Devil did it." More than likely simple physics was involved.

The complexities of the physical laws and situations that make up what happens in the world around us are usually unknown to us, and so we refer to things as happening by "chance." Why did the ball hit the window instead of the wall of the house? Why did the dice come up a nine instead of a three? Why did the toast fall jelly side down on the floor and not jelly side up? These things happen as a result of physical laws, but who can ferret through all the laws and variables? We cannot, and so we say that things happen by "chance."

"Chance" is an important part of life. Ecclesiastes notes that "time" and "chance" happen to everyone (Eccles. 9:11). Solomon told the king of Tyre that he was so blessed by God that his kingdom had rest. He did not have problems from either enemies or "misfortune" (i.e., evil chance. 1 Kings 5:4-NASB. It is the same word translated "chance" in Ecclesiastes). The Philistines had been struck by plagues after capturing the ark of God. As they prepared to send it home, they said to each other, "...If it goes up to its own territory, toward Beth Shemesh, then the LORD has brought this great disaster on us. But if it does not, then we will know that it was not his hand that struck us and that it happened to us by chance" (1 Sam. 6:9b).

How Revelation Is Given Via the Gift of Holy Spirit

When an unsaved person becomes saved, the Lord Jesus gives him the gift of holy spirit (Acts 2:33), which then becomes an integrated part of him. At the time of the New Birth (salvation), the man of body and soul becomes a three-part man of body, soul, and holy spirit (1 Thess. 5:23; Heb. 4:12). The holy spirit created inside the person fills him completely, and is in touch with every fiber of his being, both physical and mental.

Once a person has holy spirit, God or the Lord Jesus Christ can speak to him via that holy spirit inside him. God communicates with that holy spirit, which then communicates with the person's mind or body. Therefore, revelation comes through one's mind like other thoughts, or through one's body like other sensations and feelings. That is why it takes "constant use" (Heb. 5:14) to be able to accurately discern if a thought is coming into one's mind because of natural circumstances, or whether it is coming from God via the holy spirit to the mind.

When revelation comes to one's mind, it comes as a thought, emotion, or senses experience (i.e., a sight, sound, etc.). When revelation comes via holy spirit to one's body, it comes as a feeling or sensation (pain, pressure, heat, cold, etc.). The principle of how revelation works might be charted as follows:

Revelation as a thought	Revelation as a feeling
God (or Jesus Christ)	God (or Jesus Christ)
↓	↓
holy spirit in you	holy spirit in you
↓	↓
your mind	your body
↓	↓
a thought or emotion	a feeling or sensation

Once we understand that revelation usually comes as a thought or feeling we can understand why practice is so essential if we are going to reliably discern revelation from the Lord from our own thoughts and feelings.

The Seven Distinct Ways Revelation Comes to an Individual

The two categories of revelation—a message of knowledge and a message of wisdom are given in seven distinctive ways. An individual gets information from the Lord the same way he gathers information from the world around him. The Lord will give him something he can (1) see, (2) hear, (3) smell, (4) taste, or (5) touch, or sometimes he (6) "just knows." Also, the Lord may give him (7) an emotion.

When the Lord gives a person a vision, sound, smell, etc., via holy spirit, it may seem as real as if it were actually happening in the physical world, but it is happening only in his mind. Other people around him are not experiencing what he is. For example, when Stephen saw heaven open and the Lord Jesus standing at God's right hand (Acts 7:55 and 56), he "saw" it as clearly as if it had physically occurred. It was as real to him as his natural sight. Nevertheless, it was a revelation vision via the gift of holy spirit, and the others who were with Stephen did not see it. The Lord gave the revelation to Stephen via the gift of holy spirit within him, and the message went from the Lord to the gift of holy spirit to the visual center of Stephen's brain and thus Stephen "saw" heaven open. When the Lord gives revelation smell, the one receiving the revelation will smell something because the olfactory center of the brain is receiving communication from the Lord via holy spirit, but other people, even if nearby, will not smell anything.

Once we understand that revelation (i.e., a message of knowledge and a message of wisdom) comes to us by (1) seeing, (2) hearing, (3) smelling, (4) tasting, (5) touching, (6) "just knowing" and (7) emotion, we can expand the chart explaining how revelation works.

Receiving revelation works the same basic way in all seven of the ways God gives it. Because revelation information comes via the brain like the information of other thoughts and experiences, most revelation requires developing a sensitivity to it to recognize it consistently. Revelation given via holy spirit is usually a very quick experience. It usually does not "hang around" so the person can confirm it, study it, etc. It is for that reason we must become practiced in receiving revelation from the Lord. Revelation is usually a "still, small voice" (1 Kings 19:12-KJV, or as the NIV states, a "gentle whisper"). A person usually has to be quiet, peaceful, and focused to hear the voice of the Lord. Neither God nor Jesus are interested in competing with the static produced by our lack of desire and discipline. God tells us to seek Him first in our lives, and He means what He says. He will usually not "turn up the volume" to accommodate us if we do not obey His commands.

For revelation vision	For revelation sound
God (or Jesus Christ)	God (or Jesus Christ)
↓	↓
holy spirit in you	holy spirit in you
↓	↓
your mind (the visual center)	your mind (the auditory center)
↓	↓
you see a vision as if it were real[11]	you hear a sound or voice as if it were real

11. Revelation from demons works in a very similar way. When a demon inhabits a person's mind and stimulates his visual center, the person will see a vision. If it feeds information to the auditory of the brain, he will hear voices. Society acts as if people who hear voices are of an unsound mind. They are, but usually not for the reason psychiatrists think (although it is possible to see visions, hear voices, etc., because of mental illness or narcotics). Their minds are unsound because they are inhabited by demons, who are feeding visions and sounds to the person.

The Bible has many examples of revelation via seeing, hearing, smelling, tasting, touching, or knowing. We will give an example in each category:

1. **Seeing:** 2 Kings 6:17, "And Elisha prayed, 'O LORD, open his eyes so he may see.' Then the LORD opened the servant's eyes, and he looked and saw the hills full of horses and chariots of fire all around Elisha." When God gave this revelation, which was a message of knowledge by way of a vision, the servant could see the army of angels just as if it were physically there, but no one else could see it.

2. **Hearing:** 1 Samuel 9:15 and 16a (KJV), "Now the LORD had told Samuel in his ear a day before Saul came, saying, 'To morrow about this time I will send thee a man out of the land of Benjamin....'" God gave this message of knowledge by speaking it into Samuel's ear, and Samuel heard the voice as clearly as if someone had been there talking with him. It is evident from this record that most translators do not understand how revelation works, because in their versions they leave out the part about Samuel's ear, despite it being an important part of the biblical record and clearly stated in the Hebrew text.

3. **Smell:** Mark 9:25 (KJV), "When Jesus saw that the people came running together, he rebuked the foul [or "unclean"] spirit, saying unto him, Thou dumb and deaf spirit, I charge thee, come out of him, and enter no more into him." Sometimes the Lord will reveal the presence of a demon by giving the revelation of a terrible stench. Only the one receiving the revelation will smell it. Although in this record the demon may be called "unclean" as a descriptive term, it is likely that Jesus smelled a bad odor and knew that God was showing him a demon. There must have been other revelation for Jesus to know exactly what kind of demon, and that he should cast it out.

4. **Taste:** 2 Kings 4:40, "The stew was poured out for the men, but as they began to eat it, they cried out, 'O man of God, there is death in the pot!' And they could not eat it." That the men (who were prophets) spoke by revelation, and not from their five senses, is clear when the verse and its context are read and understood. The word "death" is a major key. One of the ingredients of the stew was an unknown gourd (v. 39), but when the prophet tasted the stew, he knew it was "death." Even if it tasted terrible, one would not necessarily say it was deadly. Furthermore, there is nothing in the verse that indicates the food even tasted bad. Occasionally people eat poisonous mushrooms and get sick or die because deadly food does not always taste bad. The prophets put some stew in their mouths and knew it was "death." That is a good example of how revelation by taste works. In this case, it was a message of knowledge by revelation taste. The prophets did not need a message of wisdom. Once God showed them the stew was "death," their human wisdom could guide them.

5. **Touch:** Jeremiah 1:9, The Lord touched Jeremiah's mouth. Jeremiah would have felt this revelation touch as clearly as if someone next to him had touched him. Many times when someone is ministering healing, for example, he "feels" the pain of the one he is ministering to.

6. **Knowing:** Matthew 9:4, "Knowing their thoughts, Jesus said, 'Why do you entertain evil thoughts in your hearts?'" Jesus "knew" their thoughts by revelation. This is a good example of "just knowing" what is going on. The knowledge is not specifically discernible by seeing, hearing, smelling, tasting, or touching. The person receiving the revelation "just knows" because God (or Jesus) puts the thoughts in his mind.

7. **Emotion:** 1 Samuel 11:6, "When Saul heard their words, the Spirit of God came upon him in power, and he burned with anger." When the spirit came on Saul, the result was that he became very angry. Although not all emotion, even all godly

emotion, is from the Lord, Christians should be aware that emotion can be the result of his working in them via the gift of holy spirit. Emotion is very important in the life of a godly Christian, and it can happen that God can give us an emotion via revelation, or augment an emotion we already have.

The Origin of Revelation

It is important to distinguish the "origin" of revelation from the "way," or "means by which," it comes to an individual. We have already seen that revelation comes to a person by (1) direct communication, (2) holy spirit (in a Christian), (3) demons inhabiting the person, (4) being spoken to by others in prophecy, or (5) things in the senses world such as Balaam's talking donkey. However, the "origin" of the revelation is either God (1 Cor. 2:10; 2 Pet. 1:21), the Lord Jesus Christ (Gal. 1:12; 2 Cor. 12:1; Acts 16:7[12]), the Devil (Gen. 3:1-5; Matt. 4:1-11) or a demon (1 Sam. 28:8-19; 1 Kings 22:22[13]). While the obedience and order in God's spiritual kingdom demands that no angel would give revelation without the actual source being God or the Lord Jesus, the confusion, conflict, and power struggles in the Devil's spiritual kingdom make it apparent that demons sometimes act without the Devil's permission and thus are the original source of some demonic revelation.[14]

---

12. Most textual scholars agree that "the spirit of Jesus" is the correct reading of the Greek text, rather than "the spirit" (KJV). "The spirit of Jesus" is either the genitive of apposition (i.e., "the Spirit, namely Jesus," referring to Jesus as "the Spirit" as do 2 Cor. 3:17 and Rev. 2:7, 11, 17 and 29, 3:6, 13 and 22) or the genitive of origin (i.e., the spirit given by Jesus, making reference to the fact that Jesus gave holy spirit on the Day of Pentecost (Acts 2:33) and continues to add people to his Church (Acts 2:47).
13. The true God does not send lying spirits, the Devil does. However, many people do not understand the way that God presented Himself in the Old Testament, and so have a very negative view about Him. This subject is so important that it is a major part of our book *op. cit., Don't Blame God!* by Mark Graeser, John Lynn, and John Schoenheit, Chapter Four, *"Old Testament or New Testament—Which One Is True?,"* Chapter Five, *"God Is Good (With Figures!),"* and Chapter Six, *"What About Job?"*
14. The word "angel" means "messenger." *Malak* in Hebrew, and *Aggelos* in Greek (pronounced an-gel-os), both mean "messenger." God's angels deliver messages, they are not the origin of information.

Because the origin of godly revelation is either God or the Lord Jesus Christ, prophetic messages can come from either of them. Sometimes the message clearly comes from God, sometimes clearly from Jesus, and sometimes it is unclear as to whether the source is God or Jesus. Scripture makes it clear that they work together. For example, they both send "grace and peace," as the openings of the Church Epistles testify. Many verses speak of the grace of God, but Jesus also sends grace (Rom. 16:20); God gives mercy (Rom. 12:1), and so does Jesus (1 Cor. 7:25); God blesses (Eph. 1:3), and so does Jesus (Rom. 10:12); God sanctifies (Jude 1:1-KJV), and so does Jesus (Eph. 5:25 and 26-KJV).[15] We have fellowship with both the Father and Jesus 1 John 1:3), and the basis of fellowship is communication.

There are no verses dictating whether a person will hear from God, Jesus, or both, and no verses stating that we Christians should feel more comfortable talking to God, Jesus, or both. God and Jesus are both individuals, and each seeks fellowship with Christians. It is up to each of us to develop our own personal relationship with God and the Lord Jesus, just as it is up to us to develop friendships in the physical world.

Examples of A Message of Knowledge and A Message of Wisdom in Prophecy

We have seen that revelation falls into two categories: a message of knowledge and a message of wisdom, which we will label **[MK]** and **[MW]**. Because prophecy is the communication of a message received by revelation, it follows that all prophecy also falls into the categories of a message of knowledge and a message of wisdom. The following example is the prophecy of Samuel to Saul, and it is labeled to show that God does indeed speak in these categories. A study of the prophecies in the Bible will give you a much better understanding of the way God

---

15. For more on what Jesus is doing in the Church today see our book, *op. cit., One God & One Lord* by Mark Graeser, John Lynn, and John Schoenheit, pp. 262-267. You can also visit our website www.TruthOrTradition.com.

gives information via prophecy.

1 Samuel 10:1-8

(1) Then Samuel took a flask of oil and poured it on Saul's head and kissed him, saying, "Has not the LORD anointed you leader over his inheritance? **[MK]**.[16]

(2) When you leave me today, you will meet two men near Rachel's tomb, at Zelzah on the border of Benjamin. They will say to you, 'The donkeys you set out to look for have been found. And now your father has stopped thinking about them and is worried about you. He is asking, "What shall I do about my son?"' **[MK]**.[17]

(3) "Then you will go on from there until you reach the great tree of Tabor. **[MW]**.[18] Three men going up to God at Bethel will meet you there. One will be carrying three young goats, another three loaves of bread, and another a skin of wine **[MK]**.

(4) They will greet you and offer you two loaves of bread **[MK]**, which you will accept from them **[MW]**.

(5) "After that you will go to Gibeah of God **[MW]**, where there is a Philistine outpost. As you approach the town, you will meet a procession of prophets coming down from the high place with lyres, tambourines, flutes and harps being played before them, and they will be prophesying **[MK]**.

(6) The Spirit of the LORD will come upon you in power **[MK]**, and you will prophesy with them **[MW]**; and you will be changed into a different person **[MK]**.

(7) Once these signs are fulfilled, do whatever your hand finds to do **[MW]**, for God is with you **[MW]**.

---

16. This is a message of knowledge because all that is communicated is knowledge. God does not say what to do.

17. This is a message of knowledge because all that is communicated is knowledge. Saul was never told what to do; a Bible Atlas will show that his route home was via Rachel's tomb.

18. This is a message of wisdom because God is telling Saul "what to do;" to continue on his journey even after meeting the men at Rachel's tomb. Whenever there is direction as to what to do, that is a message of wisdom.

(8) "Go down ahead of me to Gilgal. I will surely come down to you to sacrifice burnt offerings and fellowship offerings, but you must wait seven days until I come to you and tell you what you are to do" **[MW]**.

Note that in this personal prophecy Samuel gave to Saul, there is an intermixing of a message of knowledge (information, insight, and understanding from God), with a message of wisdom (direction; what God wants you to do or how God wants you to apply knowledge). Another example that clearly shows the difference between a message of knowledge and a message of wisdom is in the prophecy of Isaiah to Hezekiah when Hezekiah was sick.

2 Kings 20:1-7

(1) In those days Hezekiah became ill and was at the point of death. The prophet Isaiah son of Amoz went to him and said, "This is what the LORD says: Put your house in order **[MW]**, because you are going to die; you will not recover **[MK]**."

(2) Hezekiah turned his face to the wall and prayed to the LORD,

(3) "Remember, O LORD, how I have walked before you faithfully and with wholehearted devotion and have done what is good in your eyes." And Hezekiah wept bitterly.

(4) Before Isaiah had left the middle court, the word of the LORD came to him:

(5) "Go back and tell Hezekiah **[MW]**, the leader of my people, 'This is what the LORD, the God of your father David, says: I have heard your prayer and seen your tears; I will heal you. On the third day from now you will go up to the temple of the LORD **[MK]**.

(6) I will add fifteen years to your life. And I will deliver you and this city from the hand of the king of Assyria. I will defend this city for my sake and for the sake of my servant David **[MK]**.'"

(7) Then Isaiah said, "Prepare a poultice of figs **[MW]**." They did so and applied it to the boil, and he recovered.

Remember, when God is only giving information, that is a message of knowledge, when God is giving someone direction by telling him what to do or how to apply the information he has, that is a message of wisdom.

All prophecy is communicating what the Lord has revealed or is revealing by revelation. Therefore it is very important to understand what revelation is, how it comes, and how a person becomes sensitive to receiving it clearly and consistently. This appendix has dealt with the basics of revelation so that the student of prophecy will better understand how the one giving a prophecy received the message from the Lord that was then delivered as a prophecy.

APPENDIX E
Examples of Prophecy in the Bible

This appendix contains a partial list of corporate and personal prophecies found in the Bible to help Christians better understand and then bring forth the manifestation of prophecy. Most Christians are familiar with "corporate prophecy," i.e., prophecy that is spoken to groups. For that reason, the list of examples of corporate prophecy in this appendix is smaller than the list of examples of prophets speaking "personal prophecy," i.e., prophecy to an individual. God loves people, and He will speak to them personally or in groups. Therefore, it is important for anyone who desires to communicate God's heart to recognize both corporate and personal prophecy.

Examples of corporate prophecy (i.e., prophecy to groups)

Deuteronomy 33:1-29	Moses to the tribes of Israel
Judges 6:8-10	Unnamed prophet to Israel
2 Chronicles 15:1-7	Azariah to Asa and the people of Judah
2 Chronicles 20:15-17	Jahaziel to Jehoshaphat and Judah
2 Chronicles 24:20	Zechariah to the people of Judah
Isaiah 2:1-5:30	To Judah and Jerusalem
Isaiah 13:1-22	To Babylon
Isaiah 14:28-32	To the Philistines
Isaiah 15:1-16:14	To Moab
Isaiah 17:1-14	To Damascus (capital city of Syria)
Isaiah 19:1-25	To Egypt
Jeremiah 23:1-8	To the "shepherds" (leaders) who were destroying God's flock
Jeremiah 23:9-15	To the false prophets
Jeremiah 29:4-23	To the Judeans who were taken captive to Babylon

Jeremiah 35:18 and 19	To the family of the Recabites
Ezekiel 25:1-7	To the Ammonites
Ezekiel 25:8-11	To the Moabites
Ezekiel 25:12-14	To the Edomites
Amos 1:3-5	To Damascus
Amos 1:6-8	To Philistine cities
Amos 1:9 and 10	To Tyre
Matthew 11:21-24	Jesus to the cities of Korazin, Bethsaida, and Capernaum
Matthew 12:40	Jesus to the Pharisees about his time in the grave
Matthew 24:4-51	Jesus to his disciples about the end of the age
John 21:6	Jesus to his disciples about where to catch fish
Acts 27:10	Paul to sailors about losses if they sail

Examples of personal prophecy (i.e., prophecy to individuals)

Genesis 9:25-27	Noah to Canaan, then Shem, then Japheth about their future
Genesis 27:28 and 29	Isaac to Jacob about his future
Genesis 27:39 and 40	Isaac to Esau about his future
Genesis 49:2-27	Jacob to each of his sons
Judges 4:4-9	Deborah to Barak about war with Canaan
1 Samuel 2:27-36	Man of God to Eli about Eli's disobedience
1 Samuel 10:1-9	Samuel to Saul about being king
1 Samuel 15:1-3	Samuel to Saul about destroying the Amalakites
1 Samuel 15:16-29	Samuel to Saul about losing the kingdom
1 Samuel 22:5	The prophet Gad tells David not to stay where he was but go into Judah

2 Samuel 7:4-16; 1 Chronicles 17:4-15	Nathan to David about building a house for God
2 Samuel 12:7-12	Nathan to David about his sin with Bathsheba
2 Samuel 24:11-13; 1 Chronicles 21:9-12	Gad to David about his sin in counting Israel
1 Kings 11:29-39	Ahijah to Jeroboam about becoming king
1 Kings 13:20-22	Old prophet to young prophet about his disobedience
1 Kings 14:1-18	Ahijah to Jeroboam about his son's death and the future of Israel
1 Kings 17:1	Elijah to Ahab about the weather
1 Kings 17:13 and 14	Elijah to widow about her oil and bread
1 Kings 20:13-15, 22 and 28	A prophet to Ahab, king of Israel, about war with Syria
1 Kings 20:35-42	A prophet to another prophet and then to king Ahab
2 Kings 1:3 and 4	Elijah to Ahaziah via messengers about his death
2 Kings 1:16	Elijah to Ahaziah about his death
2 Kings 7:1 and 2	Elisha to the king of Israel and then his servant
2 Kings 8:1	Elisha to the Shunammite about a coming famine
2 Kings 8:10	Elisha to Ben Hadad via Hazael
2 Kings 9:1-10	Elisha to Jehu about becoming king
2 Kings 19:20-34; Isaiah 37:21-35	Isaiah to Sennacherib via Hezekiah about Assyria
2 Kings 20:1-11; Isaiah 38:1-8	Isaiah to Hezekiah about dying and being healed
2 Kings 20:16-18	Isaiah to Hezekiah about his relation with the Babylonians
2 Kings 21:10-15	Prophets to Manasseh, king of Judah

2 Kings 22:15-20; 2 Chronicles 34:23-28	Huldah the prophetess to Josiah, king of Judah
2 Chronicles 16:7-9	Hanani to Asa, king of Judah, about relying on Aram for help
2 Chronicles 19:1-3	Jehu the prophet to Jehoshaphat about helping Israel
2 Chronicles 21:12-15	Elijah to Jehoram, a letter
2 Chronicles 25:7-9	A man of God to Amaziah about the hired soldiers from Israel
2 Chronicles 25:15	A prophet to Amaziah about idol gods
Jeremiah 20:1-6	Jeremiah to Pashur
Jeremiah 28:15-17	Jeremiah to Hananiah about his rebellion and upcoming death
Jeremiah 34:1-5	Jeremiah to Zedekiah about his capture
Jeremiah 37:6-10	Jeremiah to Zedekiah about the fall of Jerusalem
Jeremiah 38:17 and 18	Jeremiah to Zedekiah about the fall of Jerusalem
Jeremiah 45:1-5	Jeremiah to Baruch the scribe
Ezekiel 28:1-10	Ezekiel to the king of Tyre
Ezekiel 32:1-16	Ezekiel to Pharaoh
Daniel 5:26-28	Daniel to Belshazzar about himself and his kingdom
Amos 7:14-17	Amos to Amaziah, the priest of Bethel
Haggai 2:1-5	Haggai to Zerubbabel and Joshua about being strong
Matthew 17:27	Jesus to Peter that he would find money in a fish
Luke 2:34 and 35	Simeon to Mary that a sword would pierce her soul
John 1:47	Jesus to Nathaniel about his character
John 4:17 and 18	Jesus to the Samaritan woman at Jacob's well
Acts 5:3-5	Peter to Ananias about his lies

Acts 5:9	Peter to Sapphira about her lies
Acts 13:9-11	Paul to Elymas about his stand against God and its consequences
Acts 21:11	Agabus to Paul about being bound

GLOSSARY

Anointed, anointing: In the Old Testament, kings, priests, and even occasionally prophets were publicly anointed with oil. This was a symbol of the gift of holy spirit that they were often given by God as the spiritual connection and power to do what He wanted. The gift of holy spirit was said to be "on" people (as in the NIV, NRSV) or, more accurately, "upon" them (as in the KJV, ASV, NASB). Numerous scriptures reveal this truth (cp. Num. 11:17, 25, 26 and 29, 24:2; Judg. 3:10, 6:34, 11:29, 14:6 and 19; etc.). When the gift of holy spirit was upon someone, that person was said to be "anointed" with holy spirit, as if God had poured it out of heaven onto the person. Thus the Patriarchs—Abraham, Isaac, and Jacob—are called God's "anointed ones" even though they were never anointed with oil (1 Chron. 16:22; Ps. 105:15).

The Hebrew word translated "anointed," *mashiach*, is the origin of the English word "Messiah," which literally means "the anointed one." The reason Jesus was called the "Messiah," (the "anointed one") was that he was foretold to have the spirit of God upon him (Isa. 11:2). Jesus was anointed with holy spirit (John 3:34; Acts 10:38), and he anoints each person with holy spirit the moment he is born again.

In the New Testament, as in the Old, the word "anointing" refers to having the gift of holy spirit. Each Christian receives this gift at the moment he is saved, so each Christian is "anointed" by the Lord. In the New Testament, the word "anointing" refers exclusively to receiving holy spirit at the time of the new birth (2 Cor. 1:21 and 22; 1 John 2:20).[1] Although the word "anointing" is used in many Christian circles for a special energizing or empowering by the Lord, it is never used that way in the New Testament (see "Energizing").

Charismatic: A "charismatic" Christian is one who believes in and brings forth the manifestations of the spirit (often mistakenly called "gifts of the spirit"), particularly speaking in tongues. "Charismatic" is derived

---

1. See Chapter 7, "Your Liquid Asset" in our book, *op. cit., The Gift of Holy Spirit* by Mark Graeser, John Lynn, and John Schoenheit.

from the Greek word *charisma*, "gift."

Comfort: One of the things prophecy does is comfort people (1 Cor. 14:3). The Greek word translated "comfort" is *paramuthia*, which means to comfort or to console. It can also mean to encourage, but the tenderness inherent in the meaning is such that if it were translated "encouragement" it would refer to the kind of encouragement that is in itself comforting.

Edification: The manifestation of prophecy is given for "edification" (the NIV has "strengthening," 1 Cor. 14:3). "Edification" is translated from the Greek word *oikodome*, which means "[the act of] building" or "building up." It is the act of one who promotes another's growth in the Christian walk: their godliness, wisdom, happiness, and holiness. There are other ways to build up the Church, such as the work of apostles, prophets, evangelists, pastors, and teachers (Eph. 4:11 and 12), and Christians are supposed to speak to each other in a way that builds up one another (Eph. 4:29).

Encouragement: See "Exhortation."

Energizing: "Energizing" is the biblical term for what God does when we manifest the gift of holy spirit via speaking in tongues, interpretation of tongues, prophecy, etc. God gives each Christian the gift of holy spirit and, when one steps out in faith to utilize the spirit within him, God energizes it to produce the manifestations of the spirit. Although God can give us revelation when we are not expecting it or specifically asking for it, often we must actively ask for it, step out in faith, and act. As we do, God energizes holy spirit and the manifestations are produced.

Scripture tells us there are "different kinds of working" (1 Cor. 12:6), and the word "working" is *energema*, closely related to the English word "energy." God energizes us in many different ways (Phil. 2:13). When someone manifests the spirit, he does not receive an additional outpouring of it, nor is he "anointed" with special power (see "Anointed, anointing"). When we get saved, we receive all the holy spirit we will ever receive. Then when we manifest, receive revelation, or become empowered by the Lord, it is an energizing of holy spirit with which we have already been filled (see "Filled with the spirit").

Exhortation: The manifestation of prophecy is given for "exhortation" (1 Cor. 14:3-KJV, translated "encouragement" in the NIV). The Greek word is *paraklesis,* an important word to understand because it has many meanings and applications. It is from the prefix *para*, which means "beside" or "to the side," and *kaleo*, which means "to call." *Paraklesis* is "to call to the side" which can be for a lot of different reasons. Some of its meanings and the ways it gets translated are: appeal, beseech, call for, comfort, encourage, exhort, and entreat.

It is important to understand that *paraklesis* has a wide range of meanings because the manifestation of prophecy can have varied messages, all of them being *"paraklesis."* For example, in Romans 15:4 the Word of God is to "encourage" (*paraklesis*) us so that we have hope. In 2 Corinthians 1:3, God is called, "…the God of all comfort" (*paraklesis*). God comforts in many ways. In 2 Corinthians 8:17, Titus welcomed the "appeal" (*paraklesis*) of Paul, who directed him in his caring for the church at Corinth. In 1 Thessalonians 2:3, the Apostle Paul urged (*paraklesis*) people to receive the Good News.[2] In Hebrews 13:22, the writer of Hebrews calls the book a "word of exhortation" (*paraklesis*). Among other things, Hebrews contains encouragement, comfort, appeals, and warnings. In Luke 2:25, Jesus Christ is called "the consolation [*paraklesis*] of Israel," and look at the wide variety of things he did for them. He gave them comfort, encouraged them, exhorted them, reproved them, and more.

One of the prophetic aspects of *paraklesis* is to show a person that he could be doing better than he is. Corinthians says, "But if an unbeliever or someone who does not understand comes in while everybody is prophesying, he will be convinced by all that he is a sinner…" (1 Cor. 14:24). In this record, the *paraklesis* in the prophecy

---

2. Translation "urged" by R. C. H. Lenski, *The Interpretation of St. Paul's Epistles to the Colossians, to the Thessalonians, to Timothy, to Titus and to Philemon* (Augsburg Publishing House, Minneapolis, MN, 1946), p. 241.

convinced the person he was a sinner and showed him how he could do better.

From all of the above information, we see that prophecy can comfort, encourage, be an appeal, beseech, direct, or even warn or convict. The breadth of meaning of *paraklesis* should do something for the one prophesying as well: it should beseech, direct, and encourage him to reach deep into the heart of the Lord and get everything the Lord has for that person at the time.

While we are on the subject of *paraklesis*, let us say something about the gift of holy spirit, which Jesus called the *parakletos*. In the Greek world, a *parakletos* was a legal advisor or advocate who comes forward on behalf of, or as a representative of, another. Thus the things holy spirit has been called in various versions include: the Advocate, the Comforter, the Counselor, the Encourager, the Friend, the Helper, and the more literal "another to stand by your side."

Filled with the spirit: This is one of the biblical terms for manifesting the spirit by faith, and occurs when the believer is "filled" to the point of overflowing and manifests the gift of holy spirit. A study of "filled" with the spirit, shows that it is almost always accompanied by an outward manifestation of holy spirit such as tongues, prophecy, etc. Ephesians 5:18 says to "be filled" with spirit, and this comes after 1:13, which says we have already been "sealed" by "…the promised Holy Spirit [holy spirit]." Therefore, to be "filled" with the spirit must mean more than just to have it and be a Christian. It means, "filled to overflowing" or "filled to the point of giving outward evidence."

Fruit of the Spirit: The fruit of the spirit is mentioned in Galatians 5:22 and 23. The word "spirit" refers to the spiritual nature that each believer receives the moment he is born again.[3] The fruit of the spiritual nature is the very character of Christ, the character a believer can and should develop in his life. The fruit of the new, spiritual nature is love,

3. For some of the uses of "spirit" in the Bible, see Appendix B, *"Usages of 'Spirit' In The New Testament"* in our book, *op. cit., The Gift of Holy Spirit* by Mark Graeser, John Lynn, and John Schoenheit.

joy, peace, longsuffering, gentleness, goodness, faithfulness, meekness, and self-control. God places the gift of holy spirit in each believer at the time he is born again, but that does not mean that the inner, holy nature will automatically be evident in the person's life. It will appear when he makes the effort to live like Christ lived and to put on outwardly in the flesh what has happened inwardly in the spirit. The development of the fruit is a result of both the work of the individual and of the spirit of God within him.

Inspiration: The English word literally means "in-breathing." Words and deeds are "inspired" when they are the result of God's initiative, direction, and guidance. We in Spirit & Truth Fellowship International use the word "inspiration" to refer to a person's words or actions that originate from the Lord but are spontaneous, non-cognitive, and in the moment. Inspiration refers to words or actions that do not involve any forethought, but instead are revelation from the Lord given at the same time as they are being spoken or acted out.

Judge (verb): 1 Corinthians 14:24 says that unlearned Christians and unbelievers who get a prophecy in the Church are "judged" by everyone. Most people associate the word "judge" with a negative and ungodly attitude, so it is important for us to understand what the Word of God is saying. "Judge" can be used in a good sense or an ungodly and evil sense, so any time it is used in the Bible we must determine which sense is being used. For example, Christ said not to judge (Matt. 7:1), but he also said to make a correct judgment (John 7:24). There is no contradiction because someone can judge in a good or bad sense.[4]

The Greek word translated "judge" in 1 Corinthians 14:24 is *anakrino*, and has the meanings of judge, discern, examine, or inquire. *Anakrino* is used in a negative sense when Paul says he cares very little if he is judged by others (1 Cor. 4:3). It is used in the sense of "questioned," as when Pilot examined Christ but did not find he had done anything worthy of

---

4. For more on judgment, see our booklet, *The Death Penalty: Godly or Ungodly* (Christian Educational Services, Indianapolis, IN, 2000), pp. 19-21. This booklet can be read online at www.TruthOrTradition.com TOPIC: Civil Government.

death (Luke 23:14). It is also used in the sense of being called to account, as when Peter and John were called before the Jewish leaders after they healed a crippled man (Acts 4:9). It is also used in the sense of examined or searched, as when the people of Berea "examined" (some versions have "searched") the Scripture to see if what Paul said was correct (Acts 17:11). It was not a bad thing when the Bereans examined the Scriptures; in fact, God calls them noble. Similarly, when people are prophesied to, the spirit of God searches them, examines them, and reveals the secrets of their hearts.

Manifestations: A "manifestation" is something that is clearly apparent to the sight or understanding; something that is obvious. The gift of holy spirit, like God, the Giver (who is Holy and Spirit), cannot be detected with the five senses: it cannot be seen, heard, smelled, felt, or tasted. Nevertheless, God has given nine different ways through which holy spirit becomes manifested by a believer that are clearly apparent in the senses world. The evidence of holy spirit is: a message of wisdom, a message of knowledge, faith, gifts of healing, miracles, prophecy, discerning of spirits, speaking in tongues, and interpretation of tongues (1 Cor. 12:7-10). Every Christian has the gift of holy spirit, and thus the God-given ability to utilize all of the nine manifestations, whether or not he ever does in his lifetime.[5]

Miracles: Miracles are rare and unusual supernatural acts of God that sometimes involve God superseding natural laws or the natural course of events. They are inextricably linked to God's own purposes and are an important part of His relationship with people. They demonstrate His love and support of His people, and they also glorify Him and attract people to Him. In many cases they are a response to faith and to people's need. Nevertheless, they are not the standard of truth, or even a sign that someone is walking in truth or faith. Jesus pointed out that John the Baptist, as great as he was, did no miracles (John 10:41). Because miracles

---

5. For a more in-depth explanation of each believer being able to bring forth all nine manifestations see Chapter 8, "Walking in Power: The Manifestations of Holy Spirit" in our book, *op. cit.*, *The Gift of Holy Spirit* Mark Graeser, John Lynn, and John Schoenheit. Also, visit www.TruthOrTradition.com TOPIC: Manifestations.

demonstrate God's love for people, there are many of them in the Bible. Well known biblical miracles include the parting of the Red Sea, the sun standing still, and Jesus turning water into wine. Miracles such as healing and multiplying food often give us a window into God's provision that will be abundantly evidenced in the Millennial Kingdom.[6]

Phenomenon: The dictionary definition of a phenomenon (plural = phenomena) is: "An occurrence or circumstance that is perceptible by the five senses; an unusual or significant event or occurrence." For the purposes of Bible study and clarity, when the Lord gives information in a rare, unusual, unpredictable way, that is a phenomenon. Phenomena are a subset of miracles. Miracles are supernatural acts of God, but their purpose is not necessarily to communicate information. When the sun stood still for Joshua, it was a miracle, but not a phenomenon.

The usual way that the Lord gives revelation to believers is through the gift of holy spirit, but, when he sends an angel to deliver a message, that is a phenomenon because it is unusual, unpredictable, and significant. Phenomena are God's prerogative, and He uses them for His purposes. Most often, phenomena occur in the five senses world in such a way that they are observable to anyone present. However, there are times when a phenomenon is fully perceived only by a select few present. In John 12:28-30, God spoke to Jesus from heaven, but it was not clear to the others present. Some people thought it had thundered, while others thought an angel had spoken to him.

Some biblical examples of phenomenon in the Bible are when God audibly spoke the Ten Commandments to the people of Israel (Exod. 20:1 and 19; Deut. 4:10-15, 36, 18:16; Heb. 12:19), when Balaam's donkey spoke (Num. 22:28-30), when God wrote on the wall of Belshazzar's palace (Dan. 5:1-8), at the Transfiguration when God gave Jesus and those present a vision of Moses and Elijah (Matt. 17:3-9), and when God sent an angel to speak to the Roman centurion Cornelius (Acts 10:3-7). The cloven tongues of fire that

---

6. For more on miracles, see Chapter 10, the section titled "The Role of Miracles" in our book, *op. cit., Don't Blame God!* by Mark Graeser, John Lynn, and John Schoenheit.

appeared over the apostles on the Day of Pentecost was a phenomenon because it had been foretold that Christ would baptize with holy spirit and fire, so when the fire came, the information that holy spirit had been given was aptly communicated. Phenomena happen because God chooses to communicate in some particular way something about His purposes, which may be for judgment, mercy, protection, glory, or approval.

Prophecy: Prophecy is the speaking, writing, or otherwise communicating (such as with physical illustrations or sign language) a message from God to a person or to people.[7] The noun is "prophecy," which is the thing that is spoken. The verb is "prophesy," which is the action of giving a prophecy. They are used properly in the following sentence: "In a big room, prophesy loudly or the people present will not clearly hear the prophecy."

Prophesy: See "Prophecy."

Prophet: A prophet is an individual who is specifically called to be a spokesperson for God or the Lord Jesus Christ. Although every Christian can prophesy, one with a ministry of a prophet will distinguish himself by way of the quality, quantity, and content of his prophecies. The ministry of a prophet is characterized by foretelling future events, giving divine commands and directions, reproving and correcting, and calling out ministries within the Christian Church.

Prophetic: A general term referring to the whole biblical domain of the Lord delivering a message via people who listen and respond to the spirit of God within them. The Lord can energize his spirit within people and give, or enhance, words, images, feelings, or actions that are then used to communicate his heart to others. Dreams, visions, and puzzles given via the spirit can be interpreted prophetically. Scripture was given prophetically (2 Pet. 1:20 and 21) and at times interpreted prophetically (Matt. 2:15; 1 Cor. 14:21). Teaching can also be "prophetic" when it is energized by the Lord to minister to the specific needs of a group. Witnessing can be "prophetic" when it is energized by the Lord to address the hidden needs

---

7. For more detailed information, see "What is Prophecy" in Chapter One of this book.

of a person (John 3:3, 4:7-26). Even dance, mime, and other performing art forms can be "prophetic" as they are energized by the spirit of God in the moment, showing His presence and power.

Revelation: The dictionary definition of "revelation" is "something revealed." Biblically, it means something revealed by a spiritual source. It may be from God, the Lord Jesus Christ, an angel, or from the demonic world. It may be directly from the spirit world, or it may be via a sign of some sort. A secular use of "revelation" occurs when someone learns something that helps him understand some aspect of life, but that is not the way "revelation" is used in biblical contexts. Revelation may be information that you could not know by the five senses, or it may "open your eyes" to something you already knew but had forgotten (a friendly reminder from the Lord, if you will), or never thought of in a certain way before.

Sign: A "sign" is something that points to something else. Thus, when God gives a "sign," it points to something else He wants known. The stars in the heavens are signs because they do more than just give light, they tell the story of redemption (Gen. 1:14).[8] Moses' rod that turned into a snake was a sign because it pointed beyond itself to God and to Moses as His representative (Exod. 4:8). When Jesus turned water into wine, it was more than just a friendly thing to do for a groom at a wedding, it was a sign that pointed to him as the Messiah (John 2:11), and Jesus did many other "signs" that were witnessed by the disciples (John 20:30).[9] A miracle may be a sign if the miracle points to something beyond itself.

Strengthening: See "Edification."

Wisdom: Although "wisdom" has many aspects, the *Webster's 1828 Dictionary* catches its essence: "the right use or exercise of knowledge."[10]

---

8. For more on the message in the stars, see Bullinger, *op. cit., The Witness of the Stars*.

9. For more on signs, see E. W. Bullinger, *The Companion Bible* (Zondervan Bible Publishers, Grand Rapids, MI, 1974), Appendix 176.

10. This is the first definition of "wisdom" in the facsimile reprint of Webster's, *op. cit.,* 1828 edition of the *American Dictionary of the English Language*, "wisdom."

While knowledge is "the facts concerning the case," wisdom is what to do about the situation. A good example would be Joseph in Egypt. He "knew" there was going to be a seven year famine. Wisdom dictated what to do so the people would not starve; in this case, set aside twenty percent of the harvest from the seven plentiful years before the famine struck.

Bibliography

Bach, Marcus. *Strange Altars*. The Bobs-Merrill Company, Inc., Indianapolis, 1952.

Barrett, C. K. *Black's New Testament Commentary: The First Epistle to the Corinthians*. Hendrickson Publishers, Peabody, MA, 1968.

Berry, George R. *The Interlinear Literal Translation of the Greek New Testament*. Zondervan Publishing House, Grand Rapids, MI, 1971.

Brown, Comfort, and Douglas. *The New Greek English Interlinear New Testament*. Tyndale House Publishers, Inc., Wheaton, IL, 1990.

Brown, Francis, with the cooperation of S. R. Driver, and Charles A. Briggs. *The Brown-Driver-Briggs Hebrew and English Lexicon*. Hendrickson Publishers, Peabody, MA, Sixth Reprinting 2001.

Bullinger, E. W. *The Companion Bible*. Zondervan Bible Publishers, Grand Rapids, MI, reprinted 1974.

Bullinger, E. W. *The Witness of the Stars*. Kregel Publications, Grand Rapids, MI, reprinted 1970.

Capt, E. Raymond. *The Glory of the Stars*. Artisan Sales, Thousand Oaks, CA, 1976.

Dillow, Joseph C. *The Reign of the Servant Kings*. Schoettle Publishing Company, Hayesville, NC, 1993.

Driver, S. R. *The International Critical Commentary: Deuteronomy*. T. & T. Clark, Edinburgh, UK, 1986.

Fleming, Kenneth C. *God's Voice in the Stars*. Loizeaux Brothers, Neptune, NJ, 1981.

Graeser, Mark H. *Defending Dispensationalism: Standing Fast in the Liberty*. Christian Educational Services, Indianapolis, IN, 2001.

Graeser, Mark, John A. Lynn, & John Schoenheit. *Don't Blame God! A*

Biblical Answer to the Problem of Evil, Sin, and Suffering. Christian Educational Services, Indianapolis, IN, 2006.

Graeser, Mark, John A. Lynn, & John Schoenheit. *Is There Death After Life*. Christian Educational Services, Indianapolis, IN 2004.

Graeser, Mark, John A. Lynn, & John Schoenheit. *One God & One Lord: Reconsidering the Cornerstone of the Christian Faith*. Christian Educational Services, Indianapolis, IN, 2003.

Graeser, Mark, John A. Lynn, & John Schoenheit. *The Gift of Holy Spirit: The Power To Be Like Christ*. Christian Educational Services, Indianapolis, IN, 2006.

Harris, R., G. Archer, and B. Waltke. *Theological Wordbook of the Old Testament*. Moody Press, Chicago, 1980.

Keil, C. F. and F. Delitzsch. *Commentary on the Old Testament*. William B. Eerdmans Publishing Company, Grand Rapids, MI, reprinted 1975.

Lenski, R. C. H. *The Interpretation of St. Paul's Epistles to the Colossians, to the Thessalonians, to Timothy, to Titus and to Philemon*. Augsburg Publishing House, Minneapolis, MN, 1946.

Lynn, John A. *What is True Baptism?* Christian Educational Services, Indianapolis, IN, 2002.

Morgridge, Charles. *The True Believer's Defense*. Boston, 1873. Reprinted by Christian Educational Services, Indianapolis, IN, 1994.

Schoenheit, John. *The Bible: You Can Believe It*. Christian Educational Services, Indianapolis, IN, 2005.

Schoenheit, John. *Sex and Scripture: A Biblical Study of Proper Sexual Behavior*. Christian Educational Services, Indianapolis, IN, 2000.

Schoenheit, John. *The Christians Hope: The Anchor of the Soul*. Christian Educational Services, Indianapolis, IN, 2004.

Schoenheit, John. *The Death Penalty: Godly or Ungodly*. Christian Educational Services, Indianapolis, IN, 2000.

Thayer, Joseph H. *Thayer's Greek-English Lexicon of the New Testament*. Hendrickson Publishers, Inc., Peabody, MA, reprinted 2000.

Various Authors. *The Sower* magazine, Jul/Aug 2005. Available online at www.TruthOrTradition.com TOPIC: News.

Webster, Noah. *American Dictionary of the English Language* [1828 Edition]. Foundation for American Christian Education, San Francisco, CA, reprinted 1967.

Zodhiates, Spiros. *The Complete Word Study Dictionary New Testament*. AMG Publishers, Chattanooga, TN, 1992.

[To purchase books published/reprinted by Christian Educational Services, go to www.STFonline.org/store or call us toll free at 888.255.6189 (317.255.6189), M-F 8:30 to 5 EST.]

SCRIPTURE INDEX

Topical Index

What Is Spirit & Truth Fellowship International?

Spirit & Truth Fellowship International is a worldwide community of Christians who desire to make known the written Word of God so as to proclaim the Good News of the Lord Jesus Christ. As a legal entity, we are a non-profit, tax-exempt United States (Indiana) corporation.

The fellowship and community arm of the ministry, including our events and the infrastructure (support services and finances) operates under the banner of Spirit & Truth Fellowship International. At the same time, Christian Educational Services is the publication and production arm of our ministry. Thus, our organization, like a human body, has two arms with which to reach out.

Our Vision Statement is: "A global community of committed Christians living the truth in love."

Our Mission Statement is: "To glorify the One True God and the Lord Jesus Christ by providing sound biblical teaching and a spiritually-empowered fellowship community so that all people may be saved, come to a knowledge of the truth, and become established in faithful and fruitful Christian living."

We are accomplishing our overall mission by way of live speakers, our research websites (www.TruthOrTradition.com and www.BiblicalUnitarian.com), audio and videotapes, books, and literature, as well as many different kinds of camps and conferences for all ages. Our biblically based teachings point people towards having the Lord Jesus Christ as Lord of their lives. The materials we produce are designed to assist individual spiritual growth as well as to support local fellowships and churches in the Fellowship Community. We encourage Christians to apply these teachings in their local areas in community with other like-minded believers.

We are composed of an International Headquarters and an

International network of independent local groups of Christians. This "Fellowship Community" is made up of believers who freely affiliate themselves with us because they are in agreement with our Statement of Beliefs and Code of Conduct, and have seen the quality of their lives improve by their association with us and what we have to offer. Our goal is to be a "full service" ministry where people can come and find wholeness for themselves, as well as an arena in which to exercise their own unique callings in the Body of Christ.

Our name is partially derived from Jesus' statement in John 4:23 and 24 that God is seeking people to worship Him "...in spirit and in truth." As that is the only thing stated in Scripture that God seeks, we believe it is imperative that our ministry is oriented to that way of honoring our God. We are a community of worshipers, knit together by the love of God and a common belief of His Word ("the truth"). We seek to empower each believer involved in our ministry to exercise his own unique giftings in accordance with his personal relationship with the Lord Jesus Christ.

The basis for all our efforts is the Bible, which we believe to be the Word of God, perfect in its original writing. So-called errors, contradictions, or discrepancies are the result of man's subsequent interference in the transmission of the text, mistranslations, or failure to understand what is written. We draw from all relevant sources that shed light on the integrity of Scripture, whether in the field of geography, customs, language, history, or principles governing Bible interpretation. Our goal is to seek the truth without respect to tradition or "orthodoxy."

Jesus said that knowing the truth would set one free, and our teachings are oriented to improving one's quality of life. Our goal is to provide healthy biblical teaching that helps people enjoy the fruits of salvation and authentic Christ-like living. When accurately understood, the Word of God brings great deliverance from fear, doubt, and worry, and leads the individual Christian to genuine freedom, confidence, and joy in living. Beyond such practical blessings, however, our goal is to enable

each believer to study the Bible for himself so that he is able to develop his own convictions, separate truth from error, and become an effective communicator of God's Word, and successfully live in community with other committed Christians.

What Is Christian Educational Services?

"Christian Educational Services," the original name of our ministry, is the publication and production arm of Spirit & Truth Fellowship International. This includes the research, teaching, and production of books, tapes, videos, and other study and outreach materials.

Any individual willing to examine his beliefs in the light of God's Word can profit from our teachings. They are non-denominational, and are intended to strengthen one's faith in God, Jesus Christ, and the Bible, no matter what his denominational preference may be. Designed primarily for individual home study, the teachings are the result of intensive research and rational methods, making them easy to follow, verify, and practically apply.

To receive our bimonthly magazine, *The Sower*, and a complete listing of our materials, please contact us at:

Christian Educational Services
A division of Spirit & Truth Fellowship International
2144 East 52nd Street
Indianapolis, Indiana 46205
888.255.6189 (317.255.6189), M-F 8:30 to 5 (EST)
STF@STFonline.org
www.STFonline.org

Please be sure and visit our research website: www.TruthOrTradition.com

Other Books, Publications, Seminars, and Tapes available from:

Christian Educational Services
2144 East 52nd Street
Indianapolis, Indiana 46205
888.255.6189 (317.255.6189), M-F 8:30 to 5 (EST)
STF@STFonline.org (www.STFonline.org/store)

Books

The Christian's Hope: The Anchor of the Soul – What the Bible really says about Death, Judgment, Rewards, Heaven, and the Future Life on a Restored Earth

The Bible – You Can Believe It

The Gift of Holy Spirit: The Power To Be Like Christ

Is There Death After Life?

One God & One Lord: Reconsidering the Cornerstone of the Christian Faith

Don't Blame God! A Biblical Answer to the Problem of Evil, Sin, and Suffering

Sex & Scripture: A Biblical Study of Proper Sexual Behavior

Publications

22 Principles of Bible Interpretation or How to Eliminate Apparent Bible Contradictions

Beyond a Reasonable Doubt: 23 Arguments for the Historical Validity of the Resurrection of Jesus Christ

Becoming a Christian: Why? What? How?

Righteousness—Every Christian's Gift from God

What is True Baptism?

23 Reasons to Believe in a Rapture before the Great Tribulation or Why We Aren't in the Tribulation Now

25 Reasons Why Salvation is Permanent for Christians

34 Reasons Why the Holy Spirit is Not a Separate "Person" From the Only True God, The Father

47 Reasons Why our Heavenly Father has no Equals or "Co-Equals"

Defending Dispensationalism: Standing Fast in the Liberty

The Death Penalty: Godly or Ungodly?

Audio Tape Seminars

New Life in Christ—Foundations for Powerful Christian Living (15 hrs)

The Creation-Evolution Controversy (6 hrs)

Growing Up in Christ, Part One: The Fruit of the Spirit—Developing the Character of Christ (12 hrs)

Growing Up in Christ, Part Two: Teaching and Activation in the Manifestations of the Gift of Holy Spirit (9 hrs)

A Journey through the Old Testament (26 hrs)

Romans (18 hrs)

The Book of Revelation (9 hrs)

Jesus Christ, the Diameter of the Ages (6 hrs)

Dating, Courtship, & Engagement: A Journey In Preparing For Marriage (2 1/2 hrs)

On the Errors of the Trinity (16 hrs)

We Highly Recommend This Class

New Life in Christ:
Foundations for Powerful Christian Living

(24 Sessions/15 hours. Includes a 58 page syllabus)

This class will introduce you to the foundations of biblical study and Christian living. It covers all the topics necessary to give a beginning student the tools needed to understand and apply biblical truth in everyday life. The class is a family collaboration of John Schoenheit and his sister, Sue Carlson. The blend of their two voices, manners, and teaching styles is an extremely logical and winning presentation.

Sessions:
1. New Life In Christ
2. "Take My Word for It" - God
3. "Take My Word for It" - God (continued)
4. The Text We Have Is Reliable
5. The Workman and the Perfect Word
6. Uncovering the Perfect Word
7. Uncovering the Perfect Word (continued)
8. The Fall
9. Who Is In Control?
10. Where Are the Dead?
11. Salvation and the Savior
12. Salvation By Faith
13. The Christian Church
14. The New Birth
15. The Gift of Holy Spirit
16. The Manifestations of Holy Spirit
17. Speaking In Tongues
18. Hope - the Anchor of the Soul
19. Hope - Jobs and Judgments
20. Sonship - Blessings and Responsibilities
21. Developing the Character of Christ

22. The Power of Prayer
23. Giving, Witnessing, and Fellowship
24. Praise and Worship

Related Teaching Tapes

The Manifestation of Prophecy (Sep/Oct 94)

Biblically, prophecy is speaking for God, energized by His holy spirit. In the Old Testament, prophesying was basically confined to those with the God-given office of a prophet, upon whom God had placed His spirit. Men such as Nathan spoke for God to give people direction, correction and information about God's will for their lives. Since the Day of Pentecost, everyone who believes in Jesus Christ as Lord receives the gift of holy spirit, and with it the ability to prophesy. Several times in 1 Corinthians 14, God encourages *all Christians* to speak for Him via prophecy to edify, exhort and comfort their brethren. The same specific, personal guidance from a loving heavenly Father is available today just as it has always been. This teaching gives the Scriptural basis for personal prophecy today, a way by which the power of God can deeply touch His people. By John Schoenheit.

Understanding Prophecy (May/Jun 00)

The manifestation of prophecy is very important to the Church, and that is why Satan has introduced much error and confusion about it to the end that many Christians want nothing to do with it. Prophecy is revelation in that it is what God reveals to someone in order for him to communicate to others. This teaching shows what Scripture says about it and how it is to be used properly. By John Schoenheit.

Four Keys to Evaluating Prophetic Guidance (Jan 02)

Prophecy, both personal and corporate, is one of God's provisions for the Church Age, and more and more Christians are embracing prophets and "personal prophecy." With its popularity, however, have come abuses and misunderstandings, and this teaching aims to empower the listener with the keys to evaluating all forms of prophetic guidance. Armed with this knowledge, the Christian need not fear the ministry of a prophet or even false prophets, but can separate truth from error and God's voice from the human element. How to stand responsibly in regard to a prophetic word is also discussed, in order to not bring discredit to God, the ministry of a prophet, or the manifestation of prophecy. By Karen Anne Graeser.

Recommended Seminars
Introduction to the Prophetic
Prophetic Seminar (Indianapolis, IN 1999)
(Listed under "conferences" in our online catalog)

Tape 1 - "Introduction to the Prophetic" by Karen Anne Graeser

Tape 2 - "Seek to Excel" by John Lynn

Tape 3 - "Hearing God's Voice" by Karen Anne Graeser

Tape 4 - "1 Corinthians 14: Discerning the Genuine from the Counterfeit" by Mark Graeser

Tape 5A - "Prove All Things" by Gene Speakes

Tape 5B - " Evaluating Dominion Theology and the Prophetic" by Mark Graeser

Tape 6 - "Contending for the Faith" by John Schoenheit

Tape 7 & 8A - "Questions and Answers"

Walking Courageously
Prophetic Seminar (Indianapolis, IN 2000)
(Listed under "conferences" in our online catalog)

Tape 1 - " Walking Courageously" by Karen Anne Graeser

Tape 2 - "Action Cures Fear" by John Lynn

Tape 3 - "Understanding Prophecy" by John Schoenheit

Tape 4 & 5 - "Question & Answer Session" by John Schoenheit and Karen Anne Graeser

Tape 6 - "The Genuine Vs the Counterfeit" by John Schoenheit

Tape 7 - "See it Big; Keep it Simple" by Karen Anne Graeser

Growing Up In Christ: Part 2
Teaching and Activation in the
Manifestations of the Gift of Holy Spirit

This 9-hour seminar deals with what is perhaps the most practically relevant issue in the Word of God: How does a Christian utilize the gift of holy spirit, that is, the divine nature of God and Christ with which he is endowed? How does one use the supernatural tools incorporated in this gift of life?

1 Corinthians 12:1 begins by saying that God does not want us to be ignorant about spiritual matters, in particular those that are set forth in the three chapters that follow. Obviously, the Devil wants Christians to be ignorant about those things that God wants them not to be ignorant about. Therefore, Satan has introduced many errors in regard to the gift of holy spirit and the practice of the nine manifestations of that gift. The confusion about these things currently running rampant throughout Christendom is taking its toll. Many believers' lives are suffering great trauma, and many unbelievers are ridiculing Christianity because of the chaos they can so clearly see in regard to this issue.

"Simple." "Precise." "Powerful." These are some of the terms we have heard used to describe the teachings in this package. If you think you have heard everything you could on this subject, we encourage you to think again and order these tapes. The teachings are free of any spiritual bravado, and they are not based on emotion or experience. We certainly hope you will decide to hear them for yourself, because we believe that the Lord will teach you a great deal about these vital issues. In some ways, our book, *The Gift of Holy Spirit: The Power To Be Like Christ* is a "textbook" for this seminar and, therefore, we are including it in with this package. If you already have it, we hope you will give it away to someone who has not read it. This seminar, comes with a detailed syllabus, and the teachings are as follows:

The Giver And The Gift	Discerning Of Spirits
Word Of Wisdom	Interpretation Of Tongues
Speaking In Tongues	Faith
Prophecy	Working Of Miracles
Word Of Knowledge	Gifts Of Healing

Free Indeed Video Ministry
By John Schoenheit

Each VHS Tape is Two Hours and Contains Four 30-Minute Teachings

Tape 2: Why I Believe the Bible—Prophecy (Parts 1-4)

Tape 18: The Promised Holy Spirit, The Prophetic Perfect, The Resurrection (Parts 1 & 2)

Tape 23: The Revelation and Power Manifestations (Parts 1-4)

Tape 24: The Revelation and Power Manifestations (Parts 5-8)

Tape 25: The Revelation and Power Manifestations (Parts 9-12)

For further study please visit www.TruthOrTradition.com
TOPIC: Manifestations

You can order online at www.STFonline.org/store